Damages in Investor-State Arbitration

AF705771

International Investment Law and Arbitration

Editors-in-Chief

Ian A. Laird (*Crowell & Moring; Columbia Law School; Georgetown University Law Center; International Law Institute*)
Borzu Sabahi (*Curtis, Mallet-Prevost, Colt & Mosle LLP; Georgetown University Law Center; International Law Institute*)

Managing Editor

Giovanna E. Gismondi (*Managing Director, International Investment Law Center – Georgetown University*)

Advisory Board

Brooks W. Daly (*Permanent Court of Arbitration*) – Rudolf Dolzer (*University of Bonn*) – Mark Kantor (*Independent arbitrator; Georgetown University*) – Joongi Kim (*Yonsei Law School*) – Hege Elisabeth Kjos (*University of Amsterdam*) – Andrea Menaker (*White & Case LLP*) – Antonio R. Parra (*The World Bank*) – Frédéric G. Sourgens (*Washburn University School of Law*) – Sylvie Tabet (*Trade Law Bureau, Government of Canada*) – Todd Weiler (*Independent counsel, consultant, expert, and arbritrator*) – Anne Marie Whitesell (*Professor, Georgetown University Law Center*)

Associate Editors

Paul Barker (*Barrister, Doughty Street Chambers, London*) – Nicholas J. Birch (*Stewart and Stewart*) – Kabir Duggal (*Senior Associate, Baker & McKenzie LLP; Lecturer-in-Law, Columbia Law School*) – John Laird (*Crowell & Moring*) – Diora M. Ziyaeva (*Dentons LLP*)

Volumes published in this Brill Research Perspectives title are listed at *brill.com/rpia*

Damages in Investor-State Arbitration

Current Issues and Challenges

By

Irmgard Marboe

BRILL

LEIDEN | BOSTON

This paperback book edition is simultaneously published as issue 2.1 (2018) of *International Investment Law and Arbitration*, DOI 10.1163/24055778-12340004.

The Library of Congress Cataloging-in-Publication Data is available online at http://catalog.loc.gov
LC record available at http://lccn.loc.gov/2018939534

Typeface for the Latin, Greek, and Cyrillic scripts: "Brill". See and download: brill.com/brill-typeface.

ISBN 978-90-04-36685-5 (paperback)
ISBN 978-90-04-37238-2 (e-book)

Copyright 2018 by Irmgard Marboe. Published by Koninklijke Brill NV, Leiden, The Netherlands.
Koninklijke Brill NV incorporates the imprints Brill, Brill Hes & De Graaf, Brill Nijhoff, Brill Rodopi, Brill Sense and Hotei Publishing.
Koninklijke Brill NV reserves the right to protect the publication against unauthorized use and to authorize dissemination by means of offprints, legitimate photocopies, microform editions, reprints, translations, and secondary information sources, such as abstracting and indexing services including databases. Requests for commercial re-use, use of parts of the publication, and/or translations must be addressed to Koninklijke Brill NV.

This book is printed on acid-free paper and produced in a sustainable manner.

Contents

Damages in Investor-State Arbitration: Current Issues and Challenges

Irmgard Marboe
University of Vienna, Austria
irmgard.marboe@univie.ac.at

Abstract

The assessment of damages in investor-state arbitration involves complex legal and economic considerations. Particular challenges arise from the interdisciplinary nature of this endeavor. The present issue discusses some of the pertinent specificities in investor-state disputes reflecting the tensions between sovereignty and self-determination of states and their legal obligations towards foreign investors. These tensions are primarily present in the context of expropriation, but also commitments undertaken by states in bilateral investment treaties and contracts as well as changing economic circumstances need to be taken into consideration. The lack of valuation principles that are uniformly accepted and implemented leads to uncertainty and unpredictability in practice. The present volume analyses some of the most controversial and unsettled issues, including the choice of the valuation date, appropriate valuation methods, moral damages, and the awarding of interest.

Keywords

damages calculation – expropriation compensation – bilateral investment treaties – valuation date – valuation methods – interest calculation

I Introduction

This issue of *Brill's Research Perspectives* in *International Investment Law and Arbitration* addresses recent developments and current discussions in the area of damages in international investment law. The times when this area of international investment law was the "poor cousin" in the dynamics of investment arbitration, as the late Thomas Waelde, together with Borzu Sabahi one

© IRMGARD MARBOE, 2018 | DOI 10.1163/9789004372382_002

of the pioneers in the field, once called it,[1] are definitely over. Numerous books and articles have been published in the last ten years about how to deal with the assessment of damages in international investment law and to bridge the disciplinary divide between valuation experts and lawyers.[2] In addition, the American Society of International Law and the International Council of Commercial Arbitration have created a Task Force on Damages in order to provide a forum of exchange and practical tools for arbitrators, counsel, experts, and academics for implementing the various principles, approaches and methods in practice.[3]

The present issue aims at providing additional input to the discussion in the more general framework of public international law. International investment arbitration is genuinely based in this area of law due to its legal foundation in treaties between states, so-called international investment agreements (hereafter IIAs), and the applicable norms of customary international law. It has

---

1 Thomas Waelde and Borzu Sabahi, 'Compensation, Damages, and Valuation' in Peter Muchlinski and others (eds), *The Oxford Handbook of International Investment Law* (Oxford University Press 2008) 1049, 1051.

2 Sergey Ripinsky and Kevin Williams, *Damages in International Investment Law* (British Institute of International and Comparative Law 2008); Mark Kantor, *Valuation for Arbitration* (Kluwer Law International 2008); Andrea Bjorklund, Ian Laird, and Sergey Ripinsky (eds), *Investment Treaty Law. Current Issues* III (BIICL 2009); Borzu Sabahi, *Compensation and Restitution in Investor-State Arbitration. Principles and Practice* (Oxford University Press 2011; Herfried Wöss, Adriana San Román Rivera, Pablo Spiller, and Santiago Dellepiane, *Damages in International Arbitration Under Complex Long-Term Contracts* (Oxford University Press 2014). Chapter 9 'Restitution, Damages and Compensation' in Marc Bungenberg, Jörn Griebel, Stephan Hobe, and August Reinisch (eds), *International Investment Law* (Nomos 2015) 1031 (hereafter Bungenberg and others, *International Investment Law*); John A Trenor (ed), *The Guide to Damages in International Arbitration* (Global Arbitration Review 2016) (hereafter Trenor, Guide to Damages); Florin Dorobantu, Natasha Dupont, and Alexis Maniatis, 'Country Risk and Damages in Investment Arbitration' 31 ICSID Review (2016) 219–231; Irmgard Marboe, *Calculation of Compensation and Damages in Investment Arbitration* (2nd edn, Oxford University Press 2017); Steven Ratner, 'Compensation for Expropriations in a World of Investment Treaties: Beyond the Lawful/Unlawful Distinction' 111 AJIL (2017) 7–56; Ronald Goodman and Yuri Parkhomenko, 'Does the *Chorzów Factory* Standard Apply in Investment Arbitration? A Contextual Reappraisal' 32 ICSID Review (2017) 304–325. In 2014, the Journal of Damages in International Arbitration was founded which aims 'to provide a forum for the free exchange of ideas concerning the calculation of damages, the difficulties and the challenges therein'. See J Gotanda and R Walck, 'Editors' Note' 1(1) Journal of Damages in International Arbitration (2014) v.

3 See the website of the ICCA-ASIL Task Force on Damages, available at http://www.arbitration-icca.org/projects/ICCA-ASIL-Task-Force-on-Damages.html (20 August 2017).

also certain similarities with international commercial arbitration, sharing much of the same arbitral institutions,[4] procedural rules, frequently also arbitrators, counsel, and experts.[5] References to the jurisprudence of the European Court of Human Rights, the International Court of Justice, the International Tribunal for the Law of the Sea or inter-state arbitrations as regards their valuation approaches are also present.

A notable phenomenon is that the practice of lawyers involved in investment arbitration has been divided between those who usually act in representing investors in their claims against states and those more frequently engaged on the respondent side. While this may be necessary for building up profile and expertise as well as for avoiding conflict of interest, it is sometimes detrimental to a rational discussion of the issue of damages. The lack of uniformity in the practice of tribunals may give the impression that there is no reliable guidance in calculation matters and that it remains essentially an issue of the quality of arguments and presentations who will win the next battle. This is unsatisfying from an academic perspective and for other considerations, such as predictability.

While this divide may be present also in other areas of international investment arbitration, it affects the calculation of damages in particular. In the case of jurisdiction or the scope of protection of treaty standards, a certain position might help a state in one case and strengthen the position of its investors in another. By contrast, in the area of damages, there seems to be a growing consensus that states should be protected from high damages awards. The concern of states and their counsel about being convicted to pay very high sums is not entirely supported by empirical data, which show that investors received damages in approximately 57 percent of the ICSID arbitration cases which reached the merits stage,[6] and that the average recovery rate was about 24 percent

4 With the exception of ICSID, the dedicated Center for Settlement of Investment Disputes at the World Bank in Washington, and the Permanent Court of Arbitration (PCA) in The Hague, all other arbitral institutions have their origin in commercial arbitration, amongst which notably the International Chamber of Commerce (ICC) the London Court of International Arbitration (LCIA) the Stockholm Chamber of Commerce (SCC) have been most frequently used for investment arbitration.

5 Regrettably, public international law is not yet part of the general education curriculum in many law schools. See the work of the Interest Group on Teaching International Law of the American Society of International Law (ASIL) available at https://www.asil.org/community/teaching-international-law (16 February 2018).

6 Out of a population of 201 concluded cases, only 59 reached the merits stage. 28 cases were dismissed on jurisdictional grounds, 24 were discontinued, 69 were settled, 20 did not result in a public award, and in one case the tribunal deemed the claim fraudulent. See Linda Ahee,

until 2010.[7] Even though the recovery rates have slightly increased since then, they are on average still below 40 percent.[8] The sometimes large absolute amounts are primarily due to the size of the investments involved.[9]

What remains a disturbing feature in the area of damages is the lack of consistency in arbitral practice. Several principles have come to be commonly accepted over time, but their implementation in practice remains unpredictable. Although, in the last ten years, the discussion on damages in the arbitral process and the statements of reasons by tribunals have become much more detailed and rationalized,[10] this has not changed much to the better. In this

---

Leonardo Giacchino and Richard Walck, 'Historical Analysis of ICSID Concluded Cases' 5 World Arbitration and Mediation Review (2011) 43, 44–45. These numbers are similar to those published by UNCTAD in its World Investment Report of 2015, according to which claimants won 60 percent of the decisions on the merits. See UNCTAD, *World Investment Report 2015. Reforming International Investment Governance* (United Nations 2015) 116.

7 Ahee and others, ibid., 49–50.

8 A recent study of 2017 shows that investors received damages in 58 per cent of the cases that reached the merits stage and had an average recovery rate of 39.3 percent and a median recovery rate of 32.7 per cent. These numbers were taken from a population of 385 cases of which 131 led to publicly available awards on the merits. 63 cases were dismissed on jurisdictional grounds, 73 were discontinued, 76 were settled, 34 resulted in awards that were not public, two cases resulted in annulment of the original award, and four cases involved claims that were non-monetary in nature, and in one case the tribunal deemed the claim fraudulent. See Leonardo Giacchino and Thomas Sturma, 'Trends in Awards from Concluded ICSID Cases' 4(2) Journal on Damages in International Arbitration 51, 57.

9 The award of 50 billion US dollars against the Russian Federation has so far been the record high. It is connected to the fact that the formerly state-owned company Yukos was privatised and later re-nationalised under circumstance which different arbitral tribunals have found to be expropriatory. While this alone was not particularly remarkable, the fact that the award was so high triggered a lot of discussion on the legitimacy of investment arbitration. See Mark Kantor, 'Fifty billion Dollars. The Yukos Damages Awards' 2(1) Journal on Damages in International Arbitration (2015) 91–149; Christina Beharry, 'Lawful versus Unlawful Expropriation. Heads I Win, Tails You Lose' 3(1) Journal on Damages in International Arbitration (2016) 57–97.

10 A study undertaken by PriceWaterhouseCoopers in 2015 showed that the number of pages dedicated to explaining the basis for the quantification of damages has risen from eight in pre-2000 to thirty-four pages in 2011–15. Tribunals are also addressing more complex valuation issues. See PricewaterhouseCoopers, 2015, 'International Arbitration Damages Research—Closing the Gap between Claimants and Respondents', available at http://www.pwc.co.uk/services/forensic-services/disputes/2015-international arbitration-damages-research-closingthe-gap-between-claimants-and-respondents.html; reprinted in 3(1) Journal of Damages in International Arbitration (2016) 99, 104.

situation, an appeals body, ideally on a permanent basis, could help to ensure more coherence. Unfortunately, the successful example of the WTO dispute settlement system with its ad hoc panels and a small, but permanent Appellate Body has not been taken up in recent discussions about the reform of investor-state arbitration. The "Investment Court"-system contained in the proposals for CETA and TTIP is not yet sufficiently explicit with respect to important aspects of the envisaged appeal system, such as its permanency and the number of members as well as their terms and conditions of office.[11]

For the time being, the system of ad hoc arbitration will prevail and only a thorough and open discussion of the principles and methods may add clarity, even if not necessarily predictability. The present issue will try to contribute to this discussion by addressing various aspects of the calculation of damages in investor-state arbitration. It will address legal aspects, such as the applicable law and the standards of compensation and damages, but also valuation methods and principles and their use in arbitral practice. Finally, some new developments in awarding moral damages and the important aspect of interest will be discussed.

II Special Features of Investment Arbitration in the Area of Damages

One of the key features of international investment arbitration, and a significant distinction from commercial arbitration, is that the involvement of a state or a state entity may entail considerations connected to sovereignty. States as sovereigns have certain rights and prerogatives stemming from the right to self-determination and their responsibility to safeguard public interests.[12]

11 Article 8.28 CETA leaves most of these decisions open and defers them to the CETA Joint Committee. Article 10 of the draft TTIP is more concrete (six members foreseen for the Appeal Tribunal, retainer fee as for WTO Appellate Body members) but it is more than uncertain whether this proposal will be retained. On the current discussion on the future of an investment court system see, amongst others, Catherine Titi, 'The European Union's Proposal for an International Investment Court: Significance, Innovations and Challenges Ahead', TDM 1 (2017) www.transnational-dispute-management.com; Reinhard Quick, 'Why TTIP Should Have an Investment Chapter Including ISDS' 49 Journal of World Trade (2015) 199–209.

12 See Wälde and Sabahi, 'Compensation, Damages, and Valuation' (n 1) 1056, which see investment arbitration as 'a form of international administrative law'. They suggest that this could have an effect on the calculation of compensation related to the significance and intensity of the breach. However, comparative research has not led to clear results in this respect. See Irmgard Marboe, 'State Responsibility and Comparative State Liability

On the other hand, states are also bound by the obligations they have freely decided to enter into. Most notably, IIAs are concluded to protect investors of one state from arbitrary and unlawful state behavior by another. It is therefore important to distinguish between unlawful and lawful acts of states. Not every financial disadvantage suffered by a foreign investor is compensable, but damages suffered due to a violation of a state's obligation are. What makes the proper calculation particularly difficult is that the state influences the political and economic circumstances prevailing in its territory. With this background, establishing the connection between the specific treaty violation and the damage caused is certainly not an easy task.

One of the particularities in investor-state disputes is the possibility to invoke an alleged expropriation before an international tribunal and to claim compensation or damages. The behavior of states in the exercise of their sovereign power thereby gets put under scrutiny. Also other acts of states, which are not expropriatory, are assessed in international investment arbitration, but the unique feature of expropriation is that it is not *per se* unlawful. It is recognized under general international law, and more specifically also under IIAs, that a state may expropriate foreign private property.[13] However, in so doing, the state must fulfill certain conditions, including the payment of compensation.[14] The question arises as to what extent the difference between lawful and unlawful expropriations is relevant for the calculation of compensation.[15]

Non-expropriation claims address state acts which violate one of the treatment standards foreign investors are accorded via IIAs. These typically include "fair and equitable treatment", "full protection and security", "national treatment", "most-favored nation treatment", "transfer of funds" or so-called "umbrella clauses."[16] If the state violates these obligations, it becomes responsible under international law. It needs to be analyzed to what extent it makes a difference whether an expropriation or a breach of another treaty standard occurred with

for Administrative and Legislative Harm to Economic Interests', in Stephan Schill (ed) *International Investment Law and Comparative Public Law* (Oxford University Press 2010) 377, 410–11.

13 Malcolm Shaw, *International Law*, 6th edn (Cambridge University Press 2008) 828; Rudolf Dolzer and Christoph Schreuer, *Principles of International Investment Law*, 2nd edn (Oxford University Press 2012) 98.

14 The other conditions include that the expropriation must be in the public interest, non-discriminatory and in accordance with due process. See detailed discussion further below, section E.

15 This problem is discussed further below, see section E.

16 See for a comprehensive overview August Reinisch (ed) *Standards of Investment Protection* (Oxford University Press 2008).

regard to the standard of compensation, the selection of a specific valuation method or the valuation date.[17]

The distinction between damages in expropriation versus non-expropriation cases also becomes relevant if a tribunal only has jurisdiction for either of those claims but not for both. Some bilateral investment treaties limit the jurisdiction of arbitral tribunals to issues of expropriation or to the amount of compensation in expropriation cases. Damages for other violations of the applicable bilateral investment treaty are then not covered under the jurisdictional clause of the applicable IIA. By way of example, the bilateral investment agreements concluded by the Russian Federation contain narrow jurisdictional clauses which only allow the arbitral tribunal to assess the amount of compensation, but not to decide the issue whether an expropriation occurred and whether it was lawful. Tribunals have frequently interpreted these clauses to allow them at least to assess whether an expropriation occurred, but not about the lawfulness of the expropriation and potentially higher award, as it was the case in *Quasar de Valores v Russia*.[18] Also other countries prefer such narrow jurisdictional clauses in their IIAs, as exemplified in *Saipem v Bangladesh*.[19]

On the other hand, expropriation may not fall under the jurisdiction of investment tribunals, in contrast to other breaches of the applicable investment treaty. In *Pey Casado v Chile*, the tribunal did not have temporal jurisdiction to assess the expropriation by the Chilean government in 1975, because the applicable bilateral investment treaty had entered into force only in 1994.[20] The calculation of damages should have been made on the basis of the damages caused by non-expropriation breaches of the bilateral investment treaty which the tribunal found had happened. This lack of distinction by the claimant in the re-submitted proceeding resulted in a finding of zero damages owed by the respondent, despite the numerous and varied breaches by the respondent government, and also a partial award on costs.[21]

---

17 The issue of the valuation date is addressed in detail below, section G.

18 *Quasar de Valores v Russia*, Award of 20 July 2012, SCC, para 186.

19 *Saipem v Bangladesh*, Award of 20 June 2009, ICSID Case No. ARB/05/7, para 97.

20 *Victor Pey Casado et Fondation 'Presidente Allende' v Chile*, Award of 8 May 2008, ICSID Case No. ARB/98/2, paras 420, 687–688. The award was partially annulled later mainly because of flaws in the calculation of damages, which the ad hoc Committee found had violated a fundamental rule of procedure and represented a failure to state reasons. See the Decision on the Application for Annulment of the Republic of Chile of 12 December 2012, ICSID Case No. ARB/98/2, para 287.

21 *Victor Pey Casado et Fondation 'Presidente Allende' v Chile*, Award in the re-submitted proceedings of 13 September 2016, ICSID Case No. ARB/98/2, paras 249–255. The tribunal noted that the claimants had not proved and quantified their claim to injury and damages

In the following discussion, the main legal characteristics which follow from these special features shall be examined in more detail. They have recently re-emerged as issues of controversy within topics which previously seemed to have been settled for years. The sometimes explosive political dynamics of international investment law and arbitration has revived old arguments. Amongst them figures the question on the applicable law in investor-state arbitration when it comes to the assessment of the amount of damages.

III Challenges Regarding the Applicable Law

The calculation of damages shall be guided by the law applicable to the dispute. While this seems to be obvious, the question which law is applicable with respect to remedies in investor-state arbitration is not entirely straightforward. Dispute resolution clauses in investment treaties usually refer to the treaty itself and 'applicable rules of international law'[22] or 'applicable rules and principles of international law'.[23] With respect to proceedings under the auspices of ICSID, Article 42 (1) provides:

> The Tribunal shall decide a dispute in accordance with such rules of law as may be agreed by the parties. In the absence of such agreement, the Tribunal shall apply the law of the Contracting State party to the dispute (including its rules on the conflict of laws) and such rules of international law *as may be applicable*.[24]

These provisions raise the question which rules or principles of international law are 'applicable' for the calculation of damages and compensation in international investment arbitration. As international investment treaties are 'treaties' under international law,[25] the governing law of an alleged breach is

related to breach of the BIT, but had resubmitted calculations for compensation on the basis of the alleged expropriation of their investment, which was outside the temporal scope of the applicable BIT. As a consequence, the claimants had not only received zero damages but also to bear three quarters of the total amount of the arbitration costs and their own legal costs and expenses.

22 See Art. 30 US Model BIT 2012; Art. 40 Canadian Model BIT; Art. 1131 NAFTA.

23 See Art. 18 Austrian Model BIT 2008; Art. 26 (6) ECT.

24 Article 42 (1) ICSID Convention (emphasis added).

25 As Gazzini points out: 'BITs squarely fall within the definition of treaty under Article 2 (1) (a) of the Vienna Convention on the Law of Treaties (VCLT) as they are international agreements concluded between States in written form and governed by international

'in its nature governed by international law.'[26] This is at least the prevailing view in the practice of international investment tribunals[27] and in academic writing.[28]

However, with respect to the calculation of damages the argument has recently revived that international law has developed as the law governing inter-state relations and as such could not, or at least not automatically, be applied in the relationship between private persons and states, in particular as regards the law of state responsibility and the remedies contained therein.[29]

The main argument is that Article 33 of the 2001 ILC Articles on State Responsibility states with regard to the 'Scope of international obligations set out in this Part':

> 1. The obligations of the responsible State set out in this Part may be owed to another State, to several States, or to the international community as a whole, depending in particular on the character and content of the international obligation and on the circumstances of the breach.

---

law.' Tarcisio Gazzini, 'Bilateral Investment Treaties', in: Tarcisio Gazzini and Eric de Brabandere (eds), *International Investment Law: The Sources of Rights and Obligations* (Martinus Nijhoff 2012) 99, 106.

26 Kenneth Vandevelde, *Bilateral Investment Treaties. History, Politics, and Interpretation* (Oxford University Press 2010) 445.

27 See, for example, *Amco v Indonesia*, Decision on Annulment of 16 May 1986, para 21; *CME v Czech Republic*, UNCITRAL, Partial Award of 13 September 2001, para 616; *Petrobart v Kyrgyz Republic*, SCC Case No. 126/2003, Award of 29 March 2005, paras 77–78; *Azurix v Argentina*, Award of 14 July 2006, para 50; *ADC v Republic of Hungary*, ICSID Case No. ARB/03/16) Award of 2 October 2006, paras 493–494; *LG&E v Argentina*, ICSID Case No. ARB/02/1, Award on Damages, 25 July 2007, para 31; *BG v Argentina*, UNCITRAL, Final Award, 24 December 2007, paras 427–428; *Archer Daniels v Mexico*, ICSID Case No. ARB(AF)/04/05, Award of 21 November 2007, para 280; *Gemplus v Mexico*, ICSID Case Nos ARB(AF)/04/3 and ARB(AF)/04/3, Award of 16 June 2010, paras 11.9–10, 11.12–13, 12.51, 13.79–80, 13.82–83; *Lemire v Ukraine*, ICSID Case No. ARB/06/18, Award of 28 March 2011, paras 147, 151, 155–156.

28 Dolzer and Schreuer, *Principles*, above (n 13) 17; Ole Spielermann, 'Applicable Law', in: Peter Muchlinsky, Federico Ortino, Christoph Schreuer (eds), *The Oxford Handbook of International Investment Law* (Oxford University Press 2008) 89, 107–110; Christoph Schreuer and others, *The ICSID Convention: A Commentary*, 2nd edition (Cambridge University Press 2009) Article 42, paras 193–196.

29 Martins Paparinskis, 'Investment Treaty Arbitration and the (New) Law of State Responsibility', 24 EJIL (2013) 617, 621 ff; Goodman and Parkhomenko, '*Chorzów Factory* Standard', above (n 2) 304–325.

2. This Part is without prejudice to any right, arising from the international responsibility of a State, which may accrue directly to any person or entity other than a State.[30]

The formulation 'without prejudice' should trigger a discussion to what extent consequences of a breach of international law as formulated in Part II of the 2001 Articles on State Responsibility (Articles 28 to 41) are relevant in the relation between investors and states.[31] In addition, the ILC Commentary to Article 28 raises doubts with regard to the applicability of the rules on reparation to the investor-state context, as it points out:

> Part Two has a more limited scope. It does not apply to obligations of reparation to the extent that these arise towards or are invoked by a person or entity other than a State. In other words, the provisions of Part Two are without prejudice to any right, arising from the international responsibility of a State, which may accrue directly to any person or entity other than a State, and article 33 makes this clear.[32]

This connects to the question whether the rights contained in international investment treaties are rights owed to investors or to the home state.[33] The Permanent Court of International Justice in *Factory at Chorzów* highlighted in this respect:

> The rules of law governing the reparation are the rules of international law in force between the two States concerned, and not the law governing relations between the State which has committed a wrongful act and the individual who has suffered the damage. Rights or interests of an individual the violation of which rights causes damages are always in a different plane to rights belonging to a State, which rights may also be infringed by the same act. The damage suffered by an individual is never therefore

30 Articles on the International Responsibility of States for Internationally Wrongful Acts, UN GA Resolution No. 56/ 83 of 12 December 2001, Annex (hereinafter 2001 ILC Articles).

31 Paparinskis, '(New) Law of State Responsibility', above (n 29) 635.

32 Draft articles on Responsibility of States for Internationally Wrongful Acts, with commentaries, *Yearbook of the International Law Commission*, 2001, vol. II, Part Two, Article 28, para 3 (hereinafter ILC Commentary).

33 Paparinskis, '(New) Law of State Responsibility', above (n 29) 636–638.

> identical in kind with that which will be suffered by a State; it can only afford a convenient scale for the calculation of the reparation due.[34]

The question arises what the distinction between the damage suffered by an individual compared to the damage suffered by a state from the same wrongful act may be. It can be argued that the state, when invoking the international responsibility of another state, be it by way of diplomatic protection, has a 'larger interest in maintaining the principles of international law than in recovering damages for one of its citizens'.[35] Similarly, a state can invoke responsibility 'for the loss of prestige and moral injury it has sustained and would sustain if it permitted its citizens to be injured without redress.'[36] The larger interest of the state can be the maintenance of the international legal order, based on the principle of sovereign equality of states.[37] While it may be required for the re-establishment of the equilibrium premised on sovereign equality, 'to wipe out all of the consequences of the illegal act', as required under the famous formula expressed by the Permanent Court of International Justice in *Factory at Chorzów*,[38] this might not be appropriate in investor-state arbitration.[39]

The disagreement about the applicability of the 2001 ILC Articles with regard to remedies and compensation is further supported by reference to James Crawford, the Rapporteur of the ILC on its Report on State Responsibility, who noted in 2010:

> When it comes to the intersection between investment treaties and the ILC Articles, there is a great deal of disagreement on core questions, including necessity, the application of countermeasures and issues of compensation.[40]

However, in the same article, Crawford cites numerous arbitral decisions in which tribunals as well as parties have relied on the 2001 ILC Articles and

---

34 *Case Concerning the Factory at Chorzów*, (Germany v Poland) (Indemnities) Judgment of 13 September 1928, PCIJ Series A No. 17, 28.

35 *Spanish Zone of Morocco Claims* (Great Britain v Spain) (1924) 2 UNRIAA 615.

36 *The Mavrommatis Palestine Concessions* (Greece v United Kingdom) Judgment (30 August 1924) PCIJ Series A No. 2, 12.

37 Goodman and Parkhomenko, '*Chorzów Factory* Standard', above (n 2) 319.

38 *Case Concerning the Factory at Chorzów*, above (n 34) 47.

39 Goodman and Parkhomenko, '*Chorzów Factory* Standard', above (n 2) 319.

40 James Crawford, 'Investment Arbitration and the ILC Articles on State Responsibility', 25 ICSID Review (2010) 127, 132.

applied them, in particular the provisions on reparation and compensation.[41] The 'disagreement' lies thus more in the manner and in the details of the application than in the question of applicability as such.

The 2001 ILC Articles leave the decision whether the ultimate beneficiary of rights and remedies could also be non-state entities, to the primary rules of international law.[42] Such primary rules may also contain procedures whereby non-state entities can invoke the state's responsibility on their own account without the intermediation of a state.[43] The ILC Commentary to its articles highlights the example of human rights treaties which provide a right of petition to a court or some other body for individual affected.[44] With respect to the protection of individuals under the European Convention of Human Rights, the state parties agreed to provide not only direct access to the European Court on Human Rights for a declaratory judgment, but also the right to receive 'just satisfaction', if necessary. As is well known, Article 41 of the Convention provides:

> If the Court finds that there has been a violation of the Convention or the Protocols thereto, and if the internal law of the High Contracting Party concerned allows only partial reparation to be made, the Court shall, if necessary, afford *just satisfaction* to the injured party.[45]

By contrast, under the law of state responsibility, not only 'just satisfaction', but 'full reparation' is due. As is equally well known, the 2001 ILC Articles provide:

> Article 31. *Reparation*
> 1. The responsible State is under an obligation to make full reparation for the injury caused by the internationally wrongful act.
> 2. Injury includes any damage, whether material or moral, caused by the internationally wrongful act of a State.

The ILC refers in its Commentary to Article 31 to the famous dictum of the Permanent Court of International Justice in *Factory at Chorzów*:

41 See the numerous quotes from arbitral decisions with respect to the application of Articles 31 to 36 in the form of a table, ibid., 182–194.

42 ILC Commentary, above (n 32) Article 33, para 4.

43 Ibid.

44 Ibid.

45 Article 41 of the European Convention on Human Rights of 4 November 1950, 213 UNTS 222 (emphasis added).

> The essential principle contained in the actual notion of an illegal act—a principle which seems to be established by international practice and in particular by the decisions of arbitral tribunals—is that reparation must, as far as possible, wipe out all the consequences of the illegal act and reestablish the situation which would, in all probability, have existed if that act had not been committed.[46]

The European Convention of Human Rights uses distinct language and may thus be regarded as a *lex specialis* as regards remedies available to individuals who are the victims of a violation of an international obligation by a state.[47]

As a similar situation could arise in the context of the law of international investment protection,[48] it is necessary to analyse the nature of the rights accorded to investors under bilateral or regional investment protection agreements, which are the primary law sources of international investment law.

Without going into the details about the background and rationale of international investment agreements, their main purpose is to provide a stable and reliable legal framework in order to promote and to protect foreign investments.[49] In order to achieve these goals, the agreements provide a variety of substantive standards of protection to foreign investors and, in addition, procedures for dispute settlement. It is the specificity of international investment agreements that they include procedures for disputes between investors and states in addition to disputes between states. Such direct access of investors to international dispute settlement does not only serve the purpose of providing an effective remedy to secure their economic interests, but also to de-politicize disputes between investors and host states which can pose a heavy burden on international relations.[50] The treaties also aim at balancing

46 *Case Concerning the Factory at Chorzów*, above (n 34) 47, as quoted in the ILC Commentary, above (n 32) Article 31, para 2.

47 Whether and to what extent the jurisprudence has interpreted the right to 'just satisfaction' should actually encompass 'full reparation' cannot be explored further in this context. It is true that the tendency is to assimilate the two standards, but the Court has the discretion towards a finding in this respect and/or to distinguish between different cases and to develop its own criteria thereon.

48 Yearbook of the International Law Commission, 2001, vol. II, Part Two, Article 33, para 4.

49 See, for many others, Jeswald Salacuse, *The Three Laws of International Investment* (Oxford University Press 2013) 355; Vandevelde, *Bilateral Investment Treaties* (n 26) 108–114, Dolzer and Schreuer, *Principles*, above (n 13) 20–27.

50 Sergio Puig, 'No Right Without a Remedy: Foundations of Investor-State Arbitration', in Zachary Douglas, Joost Pauwelyn, and Jorge Viñuales (eds), *International Investment Law. Bringing Theory Into Practice* (Oxford University Press 2014) 235, 251.

the rights, expectations and interests of the host state and those of the investor, at promoting good governance and the rule of law as well as at the prevention of risks and conflict. It is therefore too narrow a perspective to state that international investment treaties are merely 'designed to redress private commercial interests of investors'.[51]

The direct access to international arbitration represents a normative breakthrough with respect to the traditional treaties under international law which were concerned with regulating the relationship between states.[52] While the creation of direct rights of individuals by international treaties is not unusual,[53] the procedural rights accorded to it remain the exception. Human rights treaties are one exception, international investment agreements are another.

Sometimes, the argument is made that the substantive rules continue to apply exclusively between the parties and that investors are only granted procedural rights.[54] For the purpose of the present analyses this would only not make a difference, if the procedural rights and remedies granted to the investor would be different from those granted to the state under general international law. An answer to this question can only be found in the treaties themselves.

A difference between the rights of states and the rights of investors in investment arbitration could exist, if the applicable treaties contained specific rules on remedies that are different from those applicable between states under the law of state responsibility. The model of Article 41 for the European Convention of Human Rights shows that this would in principle be possible. However, in international investment agreements such a difference does not seem to exist. By way of example, NAFTA Article 1135, in a similar manner as several bilateral[55] and regional[56] investment protection treaties, determines under the title 'Final Award':

51 Goodman and Parkhomenko, '*Chorzów Factory* Standard', above (n 2) 319.

52 Gazzini, 'Bilateral Investment Treaties', above (n 25) 110.

53 See, for example, the rights under Article 36 of the Vienna Convention on Consular Relations, as discussed in *La Grand* (Germany v United States) Judgment of 27 June 2001, ICJ Reports 2001, 466, para 77; see also Rosalyn Higgins, *Problems and Process: International Law and How We Use It* (Clarendon Press 1994) 54.

54 Gazzini, 'Bilateral Investment Treaties', above (n 25) 111; Puig, 'No Right', above (n 50) 255.

55 See for example, Article 34 US Model BIT, Article 44 Canadian Model BIT 2004; Article 19 Austrian Model BIT.

56 Article 8.39 CETA; Article 9.29 TPP; slightly different in the formulation but similar in substance Article 26 (8) ECT.

1. Where a Tribunal makes a final award against a Party, the Tribunal may award, separately or in combination, only:
   (a) monetary damages and any applicable interest;
   (b) restitution of property, in which case the award shall provide that the disputing Party may pay monetary damages and any applicable interest in lieu of restitution.

   A tribunal may also award costs in accordance with the applicable arbitration rules.
2. [...]
3. A Tribunal may not order a Party to pay punitive damages.

There are, indeed, some differences in comparison to the general rules of state responsibility. Monetary damages are mentioned first, and restitution is available only as an alternative for the unsuccessful party which may choose between restitution and compensation.[57] The treaty thus provides some guidance how the balance between the problem of enforceability of restitution and the possible preference of a state in view of a high damages award could be solved. Secondly, punitive damages are explicitly excluded.[58] This is entirely in accordance with the general law of state responsibility, which does not allow for punitive damages, either.[59]

While Article 1135 NAFTA does not provide any further guidance on how 'monetary damages' should be calculated, it explicitly states that restitution is an available remedy, 'separately or in combination'. There is no indication that tribunals should deviate from the *Chorzów* formula which prescribes:

> Restitution in kind, or, if this is not possible, payment of a sum corresponding to the value which a restitution in kind would bear; the award, if need be, of damages for loss sustained which would not be covered

57 While restitution is often not the preferred remedy neither from the claimant nor from the respondent, the argument can be made that states would prefer to re-establish the prior situation instead of high damages claims. It should be on the respondent state's choice because enforcement of restitutions causes considerable practical and legal problems. See Christoph Schreuer, 'Alternative Remedies in Investment Arbitration', 3(1) Journal of Damages in International Arbitration (2016) 1–30.

58 The 'satisfaction' is not mentioned as a remedy explicitly can also be observed. However, tribunals have not felt prevented from making a declaration to this effect, either. They saw it as implicit power given to them. See, for example, *Victor Pey Casado et Fondation 'Presidente Allende' v Chile*, Award of 8 May 2008, ICSID Case No. ARB/98/2, para 704.

59 ILC Commentary, above (n 32) Article 36, para 4.

> by restitution in kind or payment in place of it—such are the principles which should serve to determine the amount of compensation due for an act contrary to international law.[60]

In the same vein, the 2001 ILC Articles mention restitution and compensation as two available remedies to be awarded 'singly or in combination' in order to achieve 'full reparation.'[61] The only difference between the treaty provision and the law of state responsibility is that the former leaves a greater choice to the tribunal and the respondent,[62] while the latter sets a clear priority for restitution in Article 36, para 1:

> The State responsible for an internationally wrongful act is under an obligation to compensate for the damage caused thereby, *insofar as such damage is not made good by restitution.*[63]

It still is possible that states agree on more limited remedies available to foreign investors under international investment protection treaties. It could, for example, be explored to what extent the remedies were different, if international investment law was understood as constituting a species of global constitutional and administrative law.[64]

60 *Case Concerning the Factory at Chorzów*, above (n 34) 47.

61 See Article 34 ILC Article on the 'Forms of reparation': 'Full reparation for the injury caused by the internationally wrongful act shall take the form of restitution, compensation and satisfaction, either singly or in combination, in accordance with the provisions of this chapter.'

62 The Austrian Model BIT 2008 contains an even larger choice of remedies, namely, in addition to pecuniary compensation and restitution in kind, 'a declaration that the Contracting Party has failed to comply with its obligations under this Agreement' and 'with the agreement of the parties to the dispute, any other form of relief'. This provision does not limit the tribunal's competence in awarding remedies, but brings it even more in accordance with the general principles of state responsibility. See August Reinisch, 'Austria', in: Chester Brown, *Commentaries on Selected Model Investment Treaties* (Oxford University Press 2013) 15, 45.

63 Article 31 of the 2001 ILC Articles, emphasis added.

64 Gus van Harten and Martin Loughlin, 'Investment Treaty Arbitration as a Species of Global Administrative Law' 17 EJIL (2006) 121; Stephan Schill (ed), *International Investment Law and Comparative Public Law* (Oxford University Press 2010); Santiago Montt, *State Liability in Investment Treaty Arbitration. Global Constitutional and Administrative Law in the BIT Generation* (Hart Publishing 2009).

However, current developments point into another direction.[65] The Trade Agreement between Canada and the EU (CETA), which still awaits its entry into force at the time of writing,[66] provides specific guidance towards the calculation of damages in its Article 8.39:

> Monetary damages shall not be greater than the loss suffered by the investor or, as applicable, the locally established enterprise, reduced by any prior damages or compensation already provided. For the calculation of monetary damages, the Tribunal shall also reduce the damages to take into account any restitution of property or repeal or modification of the measure.[67]

This provision reinforces the principle of 'full reparation' and the availability of restitution, but emphasizes the importance of avoiding overcompensation. While this is directed towards the protection of respondents against large damages amounts, claimants should also be protected, namely against the very high costs often involved with the conduct of international arbitration proceedings:

> The CETA Joint Committee shall consider supplemental rules aimed at reducing the financial burden on claimants who are natural persons or small and medium-sized enterprises. Such supplemental rules may, in particular, take into account the financial resources of such claimants and the amount of compensation sought.[68]

The example of CETA shows that in contemporary negotiations states are aware of the possibility to provide more explicit rules with respect to remedies and proceedings. The fact that the European states and Canada did not depart from the rule of 'full reparation' shows that it was their intention,

---

65 A comparative analysis of rules on liability of states for administrative and legislative acts, including that of the European Union, has shown that the 'administrative law'-paradigm would also not lead to a markedly different solution on the matter of remedies. See Marboe, 'Comparative State Liability', above (n 12) 377.

66 Comprehensive Economic and Trade Agreement (CETA) between Canada, of the one part, and the European Union and its member states, of the other part, Annex to the Proposal for a Council Decision on the signing on behalf of the European Union of the Comprehensive Economic and Trade Agreement between Canada of the one part, and the European Union and its Member States, of the other part, COM(2016) 444 final.

67 Article 8.39 (3) CETA.

68 Article 8.39 (6) CETA.

despite the considerable critique and opposition during the negotiations, to stay with this concept as it has been applied for decades in investor-state disputes. It remains to be seen whether this adherence will be upheld also in future negotiations, but at this moment it can be concluded that, in contrast to the European Convention of Human Rights, international investment agreements do not limit the available remedies to investors to a different standard than that provided under general international law.

IV Standards in Expropriation and in Non-expropriation Cases

Expropriation by host states has always been one of the major concerns for foreign investors. Changes in political leadership or priorities may seriously threaten the long-term enjoyment of property rights in foreign countries. Expropriation, either direct or indirect, is a means in the hands of the government to implement their political and economic choices. Frequently conflicts arise in the area of natural resources over which the countries have permanent sovereignty.[69] On the other hand, countries see the need to attract foreign capital and know-how for the exploration and exploitation of their natural resources. These tensions between safeguarding national sovereignty and attracting/protecting foreign investments are characteristic for the problems existing in the area of international investment law. At the international level, governments have had difficulty agreeing on general principles concerning the conditions for expropriation despite considerable efforts for many years.[70]

---

69 See the UN General Assembly Resolution on the Permanent Sovereignty over Natural Resources No. 1803 (XVII) of 14 December 1962 which is generally regarded as a reflection of customary international law. See Patrick Norton, 'A Law of the Future or a Law of the Past? Modern Tribunals and the International Law of Expropriation' 85 AJIL (1991) 474, 479; Salacuse, *Investment Treaties*, above (n 49) 325.

70 The failure of the Multilateral Agreement on Investment initiated by the OECD in 1998 is one of the examples of the failure of an agreement on a multilateral level. See Sornaraja, *Foreign Investment*, above (n 8) 3. Previously, the controversies about the establishment of a New International Economic Order (NIEO) also showed the lack of international consensus. See the UN GA Resolution adopting the Declaration on the Establishment of a New International Economic Order No. 3201 (S-VI) of 1 May 1974; the UN GA Resolution on the Programme of Action on the Establishment of a New International Economic Order No. 3202 (S-VI) of 1 May 1974; and the UN GA Resolution on the 'Charter of Economic Rights and Duties of States' No. 3281 (XXIX) of 12 December 1974. See for the development of the discussion, Marboe, *Calculation*, above (n 2) 46–49.

One of the first aims of international investment treaties was thus to bring clarity between contracting parties on this issue.

Expropriation has some specific characteristics which distinguish it from other treatment standards in international investment law. Firstly, expropriation is characterised by a total deprivation of the enjoyment of property rights. Whether this occurs by a formal transfer of title or not,[71] and whether the intention to expropriate or the sole effect is decisive,[72] goes beyond the scope of the present chapter. For the purpose of calculating compensation or damages it suffices to note that, once a tribunal has decided that an expropriation occurred, the investment as a whole has been destroyed, there is no prospect of the former owner to continue his/her business operations in the country, and there is no residual value to gain. This is not necessarily the case with respect to the other treatment standards.

Secondly, expropriation of foreign property as such is not prohibited under general international law.[73] International investment agreements do not change this situation and leave the sovereign right to expropriate principally untouched. Nevertheless, the level of protection of foreign property is increased by defining more clearly the conditions of expropriation. This enhances legal certainty, which is further reinforced by the possibility of dispute settlement through international arbitration.

Thirdly, expropriation is the only treaty standard which contains a measure of compensation and often also includes guidelines on how to assess the amount due, including the valuation day and interest. This characteristic feature of expropriation is frequently highlighted in international arbitration as a specificity and advantage of expropriation in relation to other treaty standards.

---

71 On the distinction between direct and indirect expropriations numerous authors have published insightful analyses in the past decades. More recent publications, with references to the earlier eminent authors, include Anne Hoffmann, 'Indirect Expropriation' in: August Reinisch (ed), *Standards of Investment Protection* (Oxford University Press 2008) 151–170; August Reinisch, 'Expropriation' in: Peter Muchlinski, Federico Ortino and Christoph Schreuer (eds), *The Oxford Handbook of International Investment Law* (Oxford University Press 2008) 407, 420–456; Ursula Kriebaum, 'Expropriation', in: Marc Bungenberg, Jörn Griebel, Stephan Hobe and August Reinisch, *International Investment Law. A Handbook* (Beck-Hart-Nomos 2015) 959, 971–981.

72 For a discussion of the expropriatory intent, the 'sole effects'-doctrine, 'police-powers', legitimate regulation and others see Ursula Kriebaum, 'Expropriation', above (n 71) 959, 982–1006; Rudolf Dolzer, 'Indirect Expropriations: New Developments?' 11 NYU Environmental Law Journal (2002) 65–93.

73 See already above (n 13).

The conditions for expropriations in bilateral treaties have developed in a largely similar way, starting in the post-World War II era with so-called Friendship, Commerce and Navigation Treaties (FCN) until the more modern Bilateral Investment Treaties, which spread particularly quickly in the 1990s.[74] Most of them are based on the well-known *Hull* formula which requires a public purpose and 'adequate, effective and prompt compensation'.[75] Also in multilateral treaties, such as in Article 13 of the Energy Charter Treaty, these conditions are reflected:

> Investments of a Contracting Party in the Area of any other Contracting Party shall not be nationalized, expropriated or subjected to a measure or measures having effect equivalent to nationalization or expropriation (hereinafter referred to as 'Expropriation') except where such Expropriation is: (a) for a purpose which is in the public interest; (b) not discriminatory; (c) carried out under due process

The requirement of 'prompt' is generally understood as 'paid without delay'. If this is not possible, an award of interest may be necessary to compensate for the delay.[76] The criterion 'effective' means 'fully realizable'.[77] Some treaties contain more specific definitions of which currencies are acceptable.[78] The payment of 'adequate compensation' is undoubtedly the vaguest criterion. As

74 Rafael Leal-Arcas, *International Trade and Investment Law. Multilateral, Regional and Bilateral Governance* (Edward Elgar 2010) 187–190; Stephan Schill, *The Multilateralization of International Investment Law* (Cambridge University Press 2009) 8–19, 40–44.

75 See the note of Secretary of State Cordell Hull to the ambassador of Mexico in 1938: 'The Government of the United States readily recognizes the right of a sovereign state to expropriate property for public purposes. This view has been stated in a number of communications addressed to your Government ... On each occasion, however, it has been stated with equal emphasis that the right to expropriate property is coupled with and conditioned on the obligation to make adequate, effective and prompt compensation.' Majorie Whiteman, *Digest of International Law, vol. VIII* (Government Printing Office, Washington 1967) 1020.

76 See on interest John Gotanda, 'Interest' in Marc Bungenberg and others (eds) *International Investment Law. A Handbook* (Beck-Hart-Nomos 2015) 1142–1153.

77 See Article 1110 (3) NAFTA: 'Compensation shall be paid without delay and be fully realizable.'

78 See Article 1110 (5): 'If a Party elects to pay in a currency other than a G7 currency, the amount paid on the date of payment, if converted into a G7 currency at the market rate of exchange prevailing on that date, shall be no less than if the amount of compensation owed on the date of expropriation had been converted into that G7 currency at the market rate of exchange prevailing on that date, and interest had accrued at a commercially

it is the reason for quite some misunderstanding and confusion, it shall be analysed in more detail.

1 *Adequate Compensation for Expropriation*

It is interesting to note that 'adequate compensation' despite its vagueness is still the most broadly used standard in international investment agreements.[79] Even though the standard allegedly claimed by industrialized states is 'full compensation', it can hardly be found in treaties.[80] To provide some guidance about what 'adequate' compensation means, treaties usually described it to a certain detail, as for example Article 1110 NAFTA:

> (2) Compensation shall be equivalent to the fair market value of the expropriated investment immediately before the expropriation took place ('date of expropriation'), and shall not reflect any change in value occurring because the intended expropriation had become known earlier. Valuation criteria shall include going concern value, asset value including declared tax value of tangible property, and other criteria, as appropriate, to determine fair market value.[81]

The World Bank in a survey and the subsequent Guidelines for the Treatment of Foreign Investment of 1992 also concluded that 'adequate' means 'fair market value':

> Compensation will be deemed 'adequate' if it is based on the fair market value of the taken asset as such value is determined immediately before

---

reasonable rate for that G7 currency from the date of expropriation until the date of payment.'

79 See the table on provisions used in international investment agreements in Ripinsky and Williams, *Damages in Investment Law*, above (n 2) 507–539.

80 The few examples which contain the standard of 'full compensation' include the treaty between Luxemburg/Belgium and Egypt of 1977 (Article V; terminated and replace by the bilateral treaty of 1999) and the treaty between Luxemburg/Belgium and the Republic of Korea of 1974 (Article 5; terminated and replaced by the bilateral treaty of 2006). The treaty between Kenia and Slovakia of 2011 is not yet in force (Article 5 contains the obligation to 'prompt and full compensation'). See, however, Muthucumaraswamy Sornarajah, *The International Law of Foreign Investment*, 3rd edn (Cambridge University Press, Cambridge 2010) 128; Matthias Herdegen, *Principles of International Economic Law* (Oxford University Press 2013) 366–367.

81 See similarly Article 8.12 (2) CETA.

> the time at which the taking occurred or the decision to take the asset became publicly known.[82]

The 'fair market value' is defined by the American Institute for Certified Public Accountants as

> the price, expressed in terms of cash equivalents, at which property would change hands between a hypothetical willing and able buyer and a hypothetical willing and able seller, acting at arm's length in an open and unrestricted market, when neither is under an obligation to buy or sell and when both have reasonable knowledge of the relevant facts.[83]

The value of an asset, under this concept, is best represented by the hypothetical price agreed between hypothetical willing buyers and sellers at the valuation date. In international valuation practice, however, the concept of 'fair market value' is not generally recognized. The International Valuation Standards Council prefers to differentiate between 'market value' and 'fair value'. The 'market value' represents a basis of valuation which is characterised as a value in exchange[84] between market participants:

> *Market value* is the estimated amount for which an asset or liability should exchange on the *valuation date* between a willing buyer and a willing seller in an arm's length transaction, after proper marketing and where the parties had each acted knowledgeably, prudently and without compulsion.[85]

By contrast, 'fair value' represent value in exchange between specific negotiating partners, namely the 'estimated price for the transfer of an asset or liability between identified knowledgeable and willing parties that reflects the

---

82 World Bank, *Legal Framework for the Treatment of Foreign Investment, Vol. 2, Report to the Development Committee and Guidelines on the Treatment of Foreign Direct Investment* (World Bank Group 1992) 31 ILM (1992) 1363, 1383.

83 See International Glossary of Business Valuation Terms, in AICPA (ed.), *Statement of Standards on Valuation Services* (American Institute for Certified Public Accountants 2015) 33.

84 As to the distinction between 'value in exchange' and 'value to the holder' see further below.

85 See 'IVS Framework' in: IVSC, *International Valuation Standards 2013* (International Valuation Standards Council 2013) 18 (emphasis in original); hereafter IVS 2013.

respective interests of those parties'.[86] As such it requires taking into consideration specific circumstances of the transaction. The International Valuation Standards Council points out:

> *Fair value* is a broader concept than *market value*. Although in many cases the price that is fair between two parties will equate to that obtainable in the market, there will be cases where the assessment of fair value will involve taking into account matters that have to be disregarded in the assessment of market value, such as any element of *special value* arising because of the combination of the interests.[87]

It follows from these definitions that 'fair market value' and 'market value' are largely synonymous. The different concept of 'fair value' would only be important in the present context, if the investment protection treaty mentioned it, which is generally not the case.[88] Most investment protection treaties use the term 'fair market value',[89] 'market value',[90] 'genuine market value',[91] 'normal market value'[92] or just 'value'.[93] Another term which is relatively wide spread is 'genuine value'[94] which is, however, not a technical term in valuation practice[95] and generally does not have a distinct meaning from market value. By contrast, the term 'real value', which is also sometimes used,[96] while not representing a technical term in valuation practice, either, might be different from market value.[97] It would need specific treaty interpretation whether this different

86 Ibid., 21.

87 Ibid., 21 (emphasis in original).

88 An exception represents the BIT between Malaysia and the Netherlands of 1971 which uses the term 'fair and equitable value' (Article 10).

89 See, for example, the Mozambique–US BIT (1998); Vietnam–Japan BIT (2003).

90 See, for example, the Indonesia–Australia BIT (1992); Chile–Australia BIT (1996).

91 See, for example, the India–Switzerland BIT (1997).

92 See, for example, the Pakistan–Japan BIT (1998).

93 See, for example, the Zimbabwe–Czech Republic BIT (1999); Nicaragua–Finnland BIT (2004).

94 See, for example, the Republic of the Congo–United Kingdom BIT (1989); Egypt–Netherlands BIT (1996).

95 Neither the AICPA nor the IVS glossaries contain an entry on it.

96 See, for example, the China–United Kingdom BIT (1986); Kazakhstan–Turkey BIT (1992).

97 The American Institute of Certified Public Accountants mentions 'real value' to explain the term 'intrinsic value' in the following way: 'the value that an investor considers, on the basis of an evaluation or available facts, to be the "true" or "real" value that will become the market value when other investors reach the same conclusion. When the term applies to options, it is the difference between the exercise price and strike price of an option

meaning was in fact the intention of the parties to the treaty.[98] The tribunal in *Rumeli v Kazakhstan* devoted some attention to the difference between 'fair market value' and 'real value', which was the applicable BIT standard for expropriated property, but came to the conclusion that '[n]o particular distinction can be drawn between 'real value' and 'fair market value'.[99]

The existence of numerous bilateral and regional international investment agreements has brought considerable certainty on the conditions for expropriation under international law. The prevailing differences in some details of the treaty provisions on compensation have not caused a lot of problems to investment tribunals. The main difficulty consists in the application of the treaty standards to the relevant facts of the case and the assessment of economic factors.

They have in common that the 'value' of an expropriated asset needs to be developed in an 'objective' way, in the sense that hypothetical market participants are chosen as the final arbiter. This is not self-evident. *Pratt* and *Niculita*, in their influential textbook on business valuation, explain that the "word value means different things to different people. Even to the same people, value means different things in different contexts."[100] The definitions of the term 'value' in the IIAs are therefore essential for giving guidance to valuation experts for the development of a meaningful valuation report. It is important in this respect to convey that the IIAs entail an objectivized, market-oriented concept of value.

Such an objective concept of value is not necessarily also prevailing in the full reparation standard under the law of State responsibility. The duty to "wipe out all the consequences" in accordance with the *Chorzów* factory dictum does not provide an indication of how the financial situation of the victim with and without the breach has to be determined. In private law, the "but-for"-principle is known as the "differential method" which is used to determine a specific type of value, the "interest", which is distinctly different from the "objective" or

---

and the market value of the underlying security.' See International Glossary of Business Valuation Terms, in AICPA (ed.) *Statement of Standards on Valuation Services* (American Institute for Certified Public Accountants, New York 2015) 34.

98 If the treaty interpretation according to Article 31 VCLT does not lead to a 'meaningful result', preparatory drafts or negotiation protocols as subsidiary means of interpretation can be used to shed some light on the issue (Article 32 VCLT).

99 *Rumeli v Kazakhstan*, Award of 29 July 2008, ICSID Case No. ARB/05/16, para 786.

100 Shannon Pratt and Alina Niculita, *Valuing a Business. The Analysis and Appraisal of Closely Held Companies* (5th edn, McGraw-Hill 2008) 41 (hereafter Pratt and Niculita, *Valuing a Business*).

"common value".[101] While the latter is the value an asset has for any person, the former is more specifically the value the asset has to the owner which represents the value the victim has the right to receive.

International valuation standards also differentiate between 'value to the owner' from 'value in exchange' and define the former as 'investment value' or 'special value'.[102] It follows that the calculation of 'full reparation', as a matter of principle, is based on different premises than fair market value.[103] It may thus also need different valuation approaches and methods. However, the rules in investor-state arbitration are not clearly defined in this respect. Tribunals enjoy the discretion to compare the 'but-for' scenario on the basis of the 'value in exchange' or the 'value to the owner'.[104]

2 *Full Reparation for Breaches of International Law*

The codification of the law of state responsibility by the International Law Commission in 2001 currently provides the most authoritative statement of the current status of customary international law as regards the legal consequences of an unlawful behavior of states. As these rules have been drafted in the context of inter-state relations, it could be argued that they are not automatically applicable in investor-state disputes.[105] However, the practice

---

101 In *Theory on Interest* (*Lehre von dem Interesse*, Schetschke und Sohn 1855, 3–18) the well-known German scholar Friedrich Mommsen elaborated the "differential method" and explained the difference between the "common value" ("Gemeiner Wert") which any person sees in an asset, and "the interest" ("das Interesse") of the particular owner. That the "differential method" is not only accepted in Germany and other civil law countries is shown in a comparative analysis in Wöss and others, *Long-Term Contracts*, above (n 2) 77–184.

102 IVS 2013, above (n 85) 17.

103 Irmgard Marboe, 'Compensation and Damages in International Law. The Limits of "Fair Market Value"', 7 Journal of World Investment and Trade (2006) 723–760.

104 See, for example, *Lemire v Ukraine*, where the tribunal emphasized that "the actual calculation of damages cannot be made in the abstract, it must be case specific." *Joseph Charles Lemire v Ukraine*, ICSID Case No. ARB/06/16, Award of 28 March 2011, para 152. See other cases distinguishing between "value in exchange" (objective-abstract value) and "value to the owner" (subjective-concrete value) in Marboe, *Calculation*, above (n 2) 88–100.

105 In particular, because the ILC's Commentary to Article 28 notes: 'Part II [...] does not apply to obligations of reparation to the extent that these arise towards or are invoked by a person or entity other than a State.' ILC, Draft Articles on Responsibility of States for Internationally Wrongful Acts with Commentaries, *Yearbook of the International Law Commission*, 2001, vol II, Part Two, as corrected (United Nations 2008) (hereafter ILC Commentary). See also the discussion by James Crawford, 'Investment Arbitration and the ILC Articles on State Responsibility,' 25 ICSID Review (2010) 1, 128, 132; Zachary

of international investment arbitration shows that the ILC Articles have been regularly referred to by tribunals and by the parties, including with respect to the question of quantum. Most importantly, the principle of 'full reparation' as reflected in the jurisprudence of the Permanent Court of International Justice in the case Factory at Chorzów has been widely referred to. In the case, the Court found:

> The essential principle contained in the actual notion of an illegal act—a principle which seems to be established by international practice and in particular by the decisions of arbitral tribunals—is that reparation must, as far as possible, wipe out all the consequences of the illegal act and reestablish the situation which would, in all probability, have existed if that act had not been committed. Restitution in kind, or, if this is not possible, payment of a sum corresponding to the value which a restitution in kind would bear; the award, if need be, of damages for loss sustained which would not be covered by restitution in kind or payment in place of it—such are the principles which should serve to determine the amount of compensation due for an act contrary to international law.[106]

The duty to 'wipe out all the consequences of the illegal act and reestablish the situation which would, in all probability, have existed' represents the core rule for the quantification of damage incurred. It has both an enabling and a limiting function and helps to avoid under- and overcompensation. This principle is contained in Article 31 of the ILC Articles on State Responsibility as follows:

> 1. The responsible State is under an obligation to make full reparation for the injury caused by the internationally wrongful act.
> 2. Injury includes any damage, whether material or moral, caused by the internationally wrongful act of a State.

The focus in investment arbitration has been on material damage for a long time, but in recent years also claims for non-material damage are raised more frequently. After the award of USD 1 million for 'moral damages, including loss of reputation' in *Desert Line v Yemen*,[107] claimants have more often raised

Douglas, 'Other Specific Regimes of Responsibility: Investment Treaty Arbitration and ICSID' in James Crawford, Allain Pellet and Simon Olleson (eds), *The Law of International Responsibility* (Oxford University Press 2009) 815.

106 *Case Concerning the Factory at Chorzów*, above (n 34) 47.

107 *Desert Line v Yemen*, Award of 6 February 2008, ICSID Case No. ARB/05/17, paras 290–291.

claims for moral damages, but without success. Investment tribunals have developed a high threshold of 'exceptional circumstances', usually implying physical threat, deterioration of health and mental suffering, or loss of reputation, credit and social position.[108]

Arbitral tribunals have applied the *Chorzów* principle by determining the financial situation of the claimant 'but-for' the breach. As the tribunal in *Lemire v Ukraine* formulated:

> But this is only a theoretical definition of a general standard; the actual calculation of damages cannot be made in the abstract, it must be case specific: it requires the definition of a financial methodology for the determination of a sum of money which, delivered to the investor, produces the equivalent economic value which, in all probability, the investor would enjoy, 'but for' the State's breach.[109]

For the calculation of damages this means that the actual and the hypothetical scenarios must be compared. Not only the breach of the state but also the likely behavior of the investor and the prevailing regulatory and economic situation in the host state must be taken into account.

The creation of a hypothetical 'but for'-scenario inevitably involves estimation and projection. Tribunals may exercise their discretion and rely on the expertise of valuation experts in their decision about which method would best lead to an appropriate and plausible comparison of the two scenarios.

3 *Contractual Damages*

Disputes between investors and states can be based on contracts concluded between them, but also in cases of IIA breaches the terms of a contract may represent the relevant basis for the calculation of damages. They create the legal framework under which the investor operates and has made its initial investment and planned its activities. Usually, investment contracts are concluded over a long period spanning over twenty or more years which renders the calculation of damages particularly complex.[110] They often involve the construction and operation of infrastructure projects, water and energy supply, waste disposal, or the exploitation of natural resources. All these activities

108 See *Siag v Eygpt*, Award of 1 June 2009, ICSID Case No. ARB/05/15; para 545; *Lemire v Ukraine*, Award of 28 March 2011, ICSID Case No. ARB/06/18, paras 326 et seq.

109 *Lemire v Ukraine*, Award of 28 May 2011, ICSID Case No. ARB/06/18, para 152.

110 As to the nature and classification of complex long-term contracts see Wöss and others, *Long-term Contracts*, above (n 2) 34–44.

are politically sensitive and prone to risk. The existence of IIAs should encourage and protect foreign investors from political risk, but it does not protect investors from economic risk.

Due to the diversity of contracts, there is not a single method of calculating damages in case of breach. Frequently, forward looking valuation methods are applied so that the contract is treated just as another investment which derives its value from future prospects.[111]

In this context, the question arises whether circumstances after the breach should or could be taken into consideration for the calculation of damages. While in some national contract laws, the foreseeability of damage at the date of the breach of the contract is decisive, under international law the aim to achieve full reparation is paramount. Several investment tribunals have therefore decided that subsequent developments and information could be included in the calculation. As the tribunal in *Amco v Indonsia* (*Amco II*) put it:

> If the purpose of compensation is to put Amco in the position it would have been in had it received the benefits of the Profit-Sharing Agreement, then there is no reason of logic that requires that to be done by reference only to data that would have been known to a prudent businessman in 1980.[112]

Also other tribunals have pointed out that there is no reason to revert to the date of the breach for the calculation of damages and included subsequent information in the calculation of damages of a long term contract.[113] Such use of the benefit of hindsight contributes to a more accurate calculation of the amount of damage actually incurred which as of the date of the award are more or less certain.[114] This view is, however, not shared uniformly.[115]

111 As to these forward-looking methods see further below, Section F.

112 *Amco Asia v Indonesia,* Award of 5 June 1990 (*Amco II*) (1993) 1 ICSID Reports 569, para 186.

113 See also *Nykomb v Latvia,* Award of 16 December 2003, ICC, 41; *El Paso v Argentina,* Award of 31 October 2011, ICSID Case No. ARB/03/15, para 710; *SAUR International v Argentina,* Award of 22 May 2014, ICSID Case No. ARB/04/4, para 263.

114 In this sense Ripinsky and Williams, *Damages in Investment Law* (n 2) 117–9; Manual Abdala and Pablo Spiller, 'Chorzów's Standard Rejuvenated: Assessing Damages in Investment Treaty Arbitration' 15 Journal of International Arbitration (2008) 103–20.

115 Wälde and Sabahi suggest using the expropriation/international law perspective for actions that qualify as governmental revocation of a contract. See Wälde and Sabahi, 'Compensation, Damages, and Valuation' (n 1) 1092, 1095.

The problem remains how to deal with the passage of time between the date of the breach and the award or the end of the contract. There is no generally accepted answer to the question whether the aggregated amount of lost revenue should be discounted as of the date of the breach, or whether should it be calculated as of the date of the award. In addition, the use of an appropriate discount rate, including for the time after the award until the end of the contract, remains an area of controversy. Valuation experts have criticized the practice of tribunals to discount the lost revenue by a high factor reflecting time value and risk, but adding pre-award interest at a low rate up until the date of the award.[116] In order to achieve full reparation also in contract cases, damages should be valued as of the date of the award which would exclude the need for an award of pre-award interest and involve less uncertainty.[117] An alternative would be the use of the same rate for calculating pre-award interest as for the discount of cash flows.[118]

V Difference between 'Lawful' and 'Unlawful' Expropriations

For a long time, the distinction between lawful and unlawful expropriations has not played an important role in international practice. Claimants were merely interested in ensuring compliance by the state with its obligations contained in the treaty with respect to compensation, nothing more and nothing less. The reason was that expropriation of property was usually equal to its physical destruction or at least the destruction of its value. If property was nationalised and put under state ownership, it generally lost its market value. In other cases, the political situation instigating the expropriation went hand in hand with the deterioration of the economic situation so that any business prospects and thus market value vanished, too. It was therefore obvious that the treaty standard providing for compensation in the amount of

---

116 Manuel Abdala, Pablo López Zadicoff, and Pablo Spiller, 'Invalid Round Trips in Setting Pre-Judgment Interest in International Arbitration' 5 World Arbitration and Mediation Review (2011) 1, 3.

117 Wöss and others, *Long-Term Contracts*, above (n 2) 284–287.

118 Ibid. Expected cash flows are generally discounted by the company's cost of equity in accordance with the DCF method. Tribunals have, however, been rather reluctant to use the costs of equity as the pre-award interest rate. An exception is *ConocoPhillips v PDVSA*, ICC Case No. 16848/JRF/CA (C-16849/JRF) of 17 September 2012, para 295.

the value of the property at the time of the expropriation was the maximum claimants could expect.[119]

However, the destruction of the property or its value is not necessarily the consequence of every expropriation. This was exemplified in *ADC v Hungary*, where the Hungarian government had directly expropriated the claimant's contractual rights to operate two terminals of the Budapest airport, but the new owners, after the privatization of the airport, could operate the airport with notable commercial success.[120] As a result, the value of the investment rose considerably after the date of the expropriation. The tribunal found that the expropriation was unlawful for various reasons, amongst others, because it did not comply with due process (as the claimants were denied of fair and equitable treatment and full security and protection) and was discriminatory.[121] The tribunal was of the opinion that, in such a case, the standard contained in the BIT for lawful expropriations should not be applied. Instead, the customary law standard for internationally wrongful acts as set out by the PCIJ in *Chorzòw Factory* should be pertinent. The tribunal seminally observed:

> The BIT only stipulates the standard of compensation that is payable in the case of a lawful expropriation, and these cannot be used to determine the issue of damages payable in the case of an unlawful expropriation since this would be to conflate compensation for a lawful expropriation with damages for an unlawful expropriation. This would have been possible if the BIT expressly provided for such a position, but this does not exist in the present case.[122]

The tribunal referred to *Phillips Petroleum v Iran* which some years earlier had noted with regard to the difference between lawful and unlawful expropriation the following:

> The tribunal believes that the lawful/unlawful taking distinction, which in customary international law flows largely from the *Case Concerning the Factory at Chorzów* (*Claim for Indemnity*) (*Merits*), P.C.I.J. Judgement No. 13, Ser. A., No. 17 (28 September 1928), is relevant only to two possible

119 Audley Sheppard, 'The Distinction between Lawful and Unlawful Expropriation', in Clarisse Ribeiro (ed), *Investment Arbitration and the Energy Charter Treaty* (JurisNet 2006) 169, 197.

120 *ADC v Hungary*, above (n 27) para 496.

121 Ibid., para 476.

122 Ibid., para 481.

> issues: Whether restitution of the property can be awarded and whether compensation can be awarded for any increase in the value of the property between the date of taking and the date of the judicial or arbitral decision awarding compensation.[123]

While the possibility of increase in value was not relevant in the situation of the Iranian revolution, in other political and economic circumstances an increase in value after the expropriation is not unthinkable, as subsequent arbitral practice showed. The tribunal in *ADC v Hungary* furthermore pointed out that the 2001 ILC Articles had closely followed the reasoning of *Chorzòw Factory* in their formulation of Article 31 (1) and in the Commentary thereon.[124] Furthermore, it referred to Article 35 of the 2001 ILC Articles and contended that restitution in kind was the preferred remedy for an internationally wrongful act, and that, according to Article 36, compensation should be awarded only insofar as the damage caused is not made good by restitution.[125] The consequence of this reasoning under the customary international law standard was that, as actual restitution could not take place, 'payment of a sum corresponding to the value which a restitution in kind would bear'[126] needed to be awarded.

Subsequent arbitral practice has largely followed the reasoning of the tribunal in *ADC v Hungary*. However, the jurisprudence is not uniform. The ICSID tribunals in *Siemens v Argentina*[127]and *Vivendi v Argentina*[128] were amongst the first who confirmed the logic to distinguish between lawful and unlawful expropriation and its consequences. Several other tribunals followed the same argument.[129] Some tribunals discussed the distinction but found that it would

123 *Phillips Petroleum Company Iran v Iran*, Award of 29 June 1989, 21 Iran–US CTR (1989) 79, para 110.

124 *ADC v Hungary*, Award of 2 October 2006, above (n 27) para 494.

125 Ibid., para 494.

126 Ibid., para 495, quoting the words of the PCIJ in *Chorzòw Factory*.

127 *Siemens AG v Argentina*, Award of 6 February 2007, ICSID Case No. ARB/02/8para 352.

128 *Compañiá de Aguas del Aconquija S.A. and Vivendi Universal S.A. v Argentina*, Award of 20 August 2007, ICSID Case No. ARB/97/3, para 8.2.3.

129 *Saipem v Bangladesh*, above (n 19) para 201; *Siag v Egypt*, Award of 1 June 2009, ICSID Case No. ARB/05/15, para 539; *Kardassopoulos and Fuchs v Georgia*, Award of 3 March 2010, ICSID Case No. ARB/05/18, para 514; *Tza Yap Shum v Peru*, Award of 7 July 2011, ICSID Case No. ARB/07/6, para 253; *Quasar de Valores v Russia*, above n 7, Award of 20 July 2012, para 215; *Hulley Enterprise v Russia*; *Veteran Petroleum Limited v Russia; YukosUniversal Limited v Russia*, Award of 18 July 2014, PCA Cases No. AA 226, 227, 228, para 1765; *ConocoPhillips and others v Venezuela*, Award of 3 September 2013, ICSID Case No. ARB/07/30, paras 342–343; *Mobil Cerro Negro v Venezuela*, Award of 9 October 2014, above

not have a relevant financial consequence.[130] An outright rejection of the relevance of the distinction is relatively rare.[131]

The need for a distinction seems thus to be increasingly, but not uniformly, recognized in arbitral practice and in academic writing.[132] The issue has considerably gained attention in the wake of the cases against Russia in the Yukos affair. The application of the above-mentioned principles lead to an amount of more than 50 billion US dollar against Russia in July 2014,[133] while an evaluation of the Yukos shares at the time of their expropriation would have only been a fraction.[134] This result was primarily achieved by moving the valuation date form the date of the expropriation date to the date of the award, due the primacy of 'restitution' under the law of state responsibility, and by adding dividends and interest on dividends from the date of the expropriation until the date of the award. According to the tribunal, in case of an unlawful expropriation, the investor should have the choice between the two dates.[135]

While several voices argue in support of the distinction and its financial consequences,[136] others are sceptical.[137] The difference in opinion seems

n 51, paras 288–189; *Tidewater v Venezuela*, Award of 13 March 2015, above n 42, para 142; *Quiborax v Bolivia*, Award of 16 September 2015, ICSID Case No. ARB/06/2, para 326.

130 *Funnekotter v Zimbabwe*, Award of 22 April 2009, ICSID Case No. ARB/05/6, para 112; *Unglaube (Marion and Reinhard) v Costa Rica*, Award of 16 May 2012, ICSID Case No. ARB/09/20, paras 306–307.

131 See, for example, *Rumeli v Kazahstan*, Award of 29 July 2008, above n 32, para 793.

132 See the arguments and cases raised against the use of hindsight information by Brigitte Stern in *Quiborax v Venezuela*, ICSID Case No. ARB/06/2, Dissenting Opinion of 7 September 2015.

133 *Hulley Enterprise v Russia, Veteran Petroleum Limited v Russia, Yukos Universal Limited v Russia*, Award of 18 July 2014, above (n 129) para 1827.

134 As the case is currently pending for national court in the Netherlands, no final determination can be made. The outcome will certainly have an influence on future decisions on unlawful expropriations.

135 *Hulley Enterprise v Russia, Veteran Petroleum Limited v Russia, Yukos Universal Limited v Russia*, Award of 18 July 2014, above (n 129) para 1769.

136 Ripinsky and Williams refer to Sornarajah and highlight that he has rightly pointed out that compensation of lawful and unlawful expropriation cannot be the same, 'for every legal system must necessarily make a distinction between damages arising from lawful and unlawful acts.' Ripinsky and Williams, *Damages in Investment Law*, above (n 2) 65; see also Marboe, *Calculation*, above (n 2) 80–84.

137 Christine Beharry, 'Lawful versus Unlawful Expropriation: Heads I Win, Tails You Lose', 3(1) Journal of Damages in International Arbitration (2016) 57–97; Floriane Lavaud and Guilherme Recenta Costa, 'Valuation Date in Investment Arbitration: A Fundamental Examination of Chorzów's Principles, 3(2) Journal of Damages in International Arbitration

to centre around the question what constitutes an 'unlawful' expropriation. One could argue that the violation of *any* of the four requirements must lead to the conclusion that the expropriation was unlawful, including the non-payment of compensation or maybe even the payment of less than the treaty standard required. According to this view, non-payment of compensation would automatically render the expropriation unlawful. As pointedly put by one author, 'the treaty provisions on compensation do not provide for the interpretive space to say that payment includes non-payment.'[138]

On the other hand, tribunals and commentators have opined that the mere disagreement over the amount of compensation and the ensuing non-payment by the expropriating state does not automatically render the expropriation unlawful. Some older cases may serve as examples,[139] as well as the jurisprudence of the Iran–US Claims Tribunal. The tribunal in *INA v Iran* found that the expropriation of the claimant's insurance company was not in violation of the Treaty of Amity between Iran and the United States of 1955,[140] but that compensation still had to be paid:

> It has long been acknowledged that expropriations for a public purpose and subject to conditions provided by law—notably that category which can be characterised as 'nationalisations'—are not per se unlawful. A lawful nationalisation will, however, impose on the government concerned the obligation to pay compensation.[141]

(2016) 33–72; Nicholas Birch, 'Curing Uncompensated Expropriation under Chorzów' 3(2) Journal of Damages in International Arbitration (2016) 73–95; Ratner, 'Beyond the Lawful/Unlawful Distinction', above (n 2) 7–56.

138 Ratner, ibid., 44–45; similarly, David Khachvani, 'Compensation for Unlawful Expropriation: Targeting the Illegality' 32 ICSID Review (2017) 385, 390.

139 *Norwegian Shipowners Claim*, Award of 13 October 1922, 1 RIAA, 307, 309, 317; *Aminoil v Kuwait*, Award of 24 March 1982, 21 ILM (1982) 967, para 115.

140 See Article IV (2) of the Treaty of Amity, Economic Relations, and Consular Rights between Iran and the United States of America of 15 August 1955: '[P]roperty shall not be taken except for a public purpose, nor shall it be taken without the prompt payment of just compensation. Such compensation shall be in an effectively realizable form and shall represent the full equivalent of the property taken; and adequate provision shall have been made at or prior to the time of taking for the determination and payment thereof.'

141 *INA Corporation v Iran*, Award of 13 August 1985, 8 Iran–US CTR (1985) 373, 378.

The tribunal considered that the 'full equivalent of the property taken' was best represented by the 'fair market value'.[142] Also in other cases, the Iran–US Claims Tribunal did not decide that the expropriations were unlawful despite the non-payment of compensation.[143]

A few tribunals under the auspices of ICSID have deemed expropriations lawful even though compensation had not been paid. In *CDSE v Costa Rica*, the tribunal decided that the expropriation was lawful and noted that 'there is no dispute between the parties as to the applicability of the principle of *full compensation for the fair market value of the Property*, i.e., what a willing buyer would pay to a willing seller'.[144] The ICSID tribunal in *SPP v Egypt*, another case of a lawful expropriation, found that 'the purchase and sale of an asset between a willing buyer and a willing seller should, in principle, be the best indication of the value of the asset.'[145]

In two cases against Venezuela, ICSID tribunals decided that the expropriations were lawful, because they only lacked the payment of compensation. The tribunal in *Tidewater v Venezuela* held:

> The Tribunal concludes that a distinction has to be made between a lawful expropriation and an unlawful expropriation. An expropriation only wanting fair compensation has to be considered as a provisionally lawful expropriation, precisely because the tribunal dealing with the case will determine and award such compensation.[146]

The applicable BIT provided for the 'market value of the investment'.[147] The tribunal referred to the above-mentioned World Bank Guidelines according to which the 'fair market value' has to be determined 'according to reasonable criteria related to the market value of the investment, i.e., in an amount that a

---

142 Which the arbitrators defined in an often-quoted formulation as follows: 'Fair market value' may be stated as the amount which a willing buyer would have paid to a willing seller for the shares of a going concern, disregarding any diminution of value due to the nationalisation itself or the anticipation thereof, and excluding consideration of events thereafter that might have increased or decreased the value of the shares. Ibid., 379.

143 *American International Group v Iran*, 4 Iran–US CTR (1983) 96, 106; *Amoco International Finance v Iran*, Award of 14 July 1987, 15 Iran–US CTR (1987) 189, para 147; see also Charles Brower and Juergen Brueschke, *The Iran–US Claims Tribunal* (Martinus Nijhoff 1999) 499.

144 *CDSE v Costa Rica*, Award of 17 February 2000, ICSID Case No. ARB/96/1, para 73 (emphasis in original).

145 *SPP v Egypt*, Award of 20 May 1992, ICSID Case No. ARB/84/3, para 197.

146 *Tidewater v Venezuela*, above (n 129) para 141.

147 See Article 5 of the Barbados–Venezuela BIT (1994).

willing buyer would normally pay to a willing seller'.[148] The tribunal contented that this standard was also required by customary international law.[149]

In *Venezuela Holdings v Venezuela*, the tribunal found, in the same vein, that 'the mere fact that an investor had not received compensation does not itself render an expropriation unlawful.'[150] It applied the BIT standard which was 'just compensation' as defined as 'the market value of the investments affected [and] correspond to the amount that a willing buyer would have been ready to pay to a willing seller at the time.'[151]

However, as compensation is one of the conditions for a lawful expropriation, the payment or non-payment cannot be totally irrelevant. The behaviour of the state, whether it accepts or rejects the obligation to pay as such, or whether it took concrete steps to this effect, needs to be taken into consideration. If the state has made efforts to pay compensation, has started negotiations, has established a commission to determine the amount of compensation, or has made an offer of compensation in good faith, the state should not be blamed for unlawful behaviour, even if it has not paid compensation.[152] As Judge Brower formulated in his Separate Opinion in *Sedco v NIOC*:

---

148 *Tidewater v Venezuela*, above (n 129) para 154.

149 Ibid., para 152. This is, however, doubtful. The World Bank in its survey of 1992 only attempted to identify and formulate general principles which may represent a basis for further development of customary international law in this area. World Bank, *Legal Framework*, above (n 82) 1370. It is not clear whether state practice and *opinio iuris* has developed in the past 25 years in a way that has put the requirement of 'prompt, adequate, and effective' compensation beyond dispute. The test case could have been Venezuela with its socialist policy aiming at the nationalisation of the natural resource industry. However, all cases against Venezuela were based on BITs so that they cannot be taken as evidence for an emerging practice and *opinio iuris*. Perhaps several pronouncements of Huge Chavez in the context of his 'Bolivarian Revolution' could be taken as *opinio iuris* at least of Venezuela. They indicate that Chavez did not maintain that nationalisations of foreign investors could be made without any compensation. However, they were too unspecific as to discern any particular standard of compensation.

150 *Venezuela Holdings v Venezuela*, Award of 2 October 2015, ICSID Case No. ARB/07/27, para 301.

151 See Article 6 of the applicable Netherlands–Venezuela BIT (1991). *Venezuela Holdings v Venezuela*, Award of 2 October 2015, ICSID Case No. ARB/07/27, para 307.

152 In *INA v Iran*, the efforts of the Iranian Government for the establishment of a committee which should decide about the amount due were apparently sufficient to convince the tribunal of the state's intention to pay compensation and thus of the lawfulness of the expropriation. See *INA Corporation v Iran*, above (n 141) 378. The same was true in *American International Group v Iran*, where the valuation of another insurance company was at issue. See *American International Group v Iran*, Award of 19 December 1983,

> I must express doubt as to whether, under customary international law, a State's mere failure, in the end, actually to have compensated in accordance with the international law standard set forth herein necessarily renders the underlying taking ipso facto wrongful. If, for example, contemporaneously with the taking the expropriating State provides a means for the determination of compensation which on its face appears calculated to result in the required compensation ... it would appear appropriate not to find that the taking itself was unlawful but rather only to conclude that the independent obligation to compensate has not been satisfied.[153]

Eminent authors seem to agree that the mere lack of compensation does not lead to the unlawfulness of the expropriation.[154]

On the other hand, the international responsibility of a state does not depend on subjective aspects of state behaviour, such as the acceptance or rejection of a certain obligation, and if the steps taken towards the assessment of compensation do not lead to a result, the conditions for a lawful expropriation are simply not fulfilled. If can therefore also be argued that the non-payment of compensation renders the expropriation necessarily unlawful. In such a case, the state commits an unlawful act and the rules on state responsibility need to be applied.

Does this necessarily lead to the primacy of restitution and the valuation of the investment at the date of the award at the choice of the investor? The *Chorzów* principle and the 'full reparation'-standard require the creation of a counter factual scenario—the situation without the illegal act—which involves numerous facts and assumptions. Most importantly, the causal link between the damage and the scope of protection of the legal norm which was violated needs to be considered. This enables a distinction between lawful and unlawful aspects of the expropriatory act of the state and to evaluate the damage accordingly.[155] If only compensation was not paid, but all other

4 Iran–US CTR (1983) 96, 106. See also *Amoco International Finance v Iran*, above (n 143) para 147.

153 *Sedco Inc v NIOC*, Separate Opinion Brower, 10 Iran–US CTR (1986) 189, 204.

154 See August Reinisch, 'Legality of Expropriations' in: August Reinisch (ed) *Standards of Investment Protection* (Oxford University Press 2008) 171, 199; Ripinsky and Williams, *Damages in Investment Law*, above (n 2) 68–69; James Crawford, *Brownlie's Principles of International Law* (Oxford University Press 2012) 624; Georg Schwarzenberger, *International Law as Applied by International Tribunals* (Stevens and Sons 1957) 666.

155 See Khachvani, 'Targeting Illegality', above (n 138) 394.

conditions of the expropriation are met, the expropriation as such seems to be legitimate, but not 'lawful' in a legal sense.[156] If the expropriation itself is for a public purpose, non-discriminatory and in accordance with due process of law, expropriation should not be based on a counter factual scenario in which no expropriation occurred. Instead, the injured party should be put in the situation it would be in, if a lawful expropriation had occurred.[157] This means, reparation would be equivalent to the compensation required under the treaty, i.e. the value of the expropriated property at the time of the expropriation, increased by an appropriate award of interest. The Iran–US Claims Tribunal, in *Amoco International Finance v Iran*, has already proposed such a solution and found a correct interpretation of the *Chorzów* standard in this respect to be 'of paramount importance':

> It means that the compensation to be paid in a case of a lawful expropriation (or of a taking which lacks only the payment of a fair compensation to be lawful) is limited to the value of the undertaking at the moment of dispossession, i.e. 'the price of what was expropriated'.[158]

Even though this concept has not been consistently pursued in subsequent cases of the Iran–US Claims Tribunal,[159] such an approach could bridge the diverging opinions between the applicability or not of the *Chorzów* standard in investor-state disputes on expropriation and still allow for differentiation between various degrees of unlawful conduct.[160]

Compliance with the criteria of public purpose, non-discrimination and due process is therefore of particular importance when deciding whether enhanced reparation might be sought under the *Chorzów* standard in comparison with the treaty standard. If expropriations are not in compliance with these

156 This is important also because most investment tribunals only have jurisdiction for alleged 'breaches' of it (see for example Article 1116 NAFTA). The tribunal can therefore not decide that the agreement was not breached but still order compensation. See Khachvani, ibid., 389.

157 Ibid., 395; see similarly Birch, 'Curing Uncompensated Expropriation', above (n 104) 94; Lavaud and Costa, 'Valuation Date', above (n 137) 71–72.

158 *Amoco International Finance v Iran*, above (n 143) para 196.

159 Brower and Brueschke, *Iran–US Claims Tribunal*, above (n 143) 499.

160 A more refined application, which reflects the causation between the unlawful acts and the damage more precisely, will lead to results that are consistent with the law as it has developed over the years and lead to better reasoned results. This is preferable to a rejection of the *Chorzów* standard altogether. See, however, Ratner, 'Beyond the Lawful/Unlawful Distinction', above (n 2) 28.

conditions, it can be argued that the expropriation should not have taken place at all. Reparation must then 'wipe out' all the consequences of the expropriation and the re-establish the situation that would exist is the expropriation had not occurred. In this case, the primacy of restitution mandates that the property has to be restituted. If this is not feasible, not practicable or not sufficient, compensation should be calculated so as to achieve as much as possible the financial *restitution in integrum.* The minimum to be awarded is the standard of compensation as laid down for lawful expropriations in the applicable treaty, i.e. the value of the investment at the time of the expropriation plus interest up to the day of the award, because compensation for an unlawful expropriation cannot be less than that for a lawful expropriation. As it might not be certain, whether the value of the investment has increased or decreased since the expropriation, the investor has the choice between the two valuation dates.[161] In addition, damages incurred since the time of the expropriation must be compensated as far as this is necessary to repair the damage caused by the unlawful act.[162] There are many different ways of achieving full reparation after an unlawful expropriation. The facts of every case need to be reflected upon so that the scenario with and without the unlawful acts can be compared. No more than the damage actually caused by the unlawful acts shall be awarded. An undyed application of these principles will avoid overcompensation.

The issue of how to deal with an increase in value of the expropriated property has been the reason for the controversial debate on compensation for expropriation in recent years. To some, it seemed arbitrary that the outcome of an award should depend on the date of the end of the arbitration proceedings, as external factors, such as commodity prices or the general economic situation in a country, which are entirely unrelated to the unlawful act, would have a significant impact on the amount of the award.[163] However, an increase in value has been rare in the past and may well remain rare in the future. The few outliers, where tribunals awarded the higher value at the date of the award,[164] and where some details in the calculation were perhaps not entirely

161 See *Hulley Enterprise v Russia, Veteran Petroleum Limited v Russia, YukosUniversal Limited v Russia*, Award of 18 July 2014, above (n 129) para 1763.

162 See Art. 36 (1) ILC Articles: "... compensate for the damage caused thereby, insofar as such damage is not made good by restituition."

163 See Stern, Dissenting Opinion in *Quiborax v Bolivia*, above (n 132) 28.

164 Brigitte Stern in her Dissenting Opinion in *Quiborax v Bolivia* referred to these cases as an 'ultraminority position'. See Stern, ibid., 12. However, out of the four cases she mentions, only two have actually resulted in damages representing the higher value at the date of the award, namely *ADC v Hungary* and *Hulley Enterprises, Veteran Petroleum and Yukos v Russia*. In *Siemens v Argentina*, the value was not higher at the date of the award than at

convincing,[165] do not justify putting into question the above mentioned recognized principles under the law of state responsibility.

VI Causation

Causation is an essential element for the quantification of damage. It represents the link between the wrongful act and the injury. Only damage *caused* is recoverable. However, it has to be pointed out that factual causation is necessary, but not sufficient. In addition to the fact that the wrongful act had some influences to the occurrence of damage—as a *conditio sine qua non*—it is important that it is legally connected to the damage. In other words, the damage has to fall within the ambit of the legal norm violated with regard to its purpose.[166] The relevant causation therefore depends on the legal norm.

Under the ILC Articles on State Responsibility, the responsible state is obliged to make full reparation for 'the injury caused by the internationally wrongful act'[167] and that compensation shall cover any financially assessable damage including loss of profits 'insofar as it is established'.[168] The ILC Commentary notes that there are various concepts used to describe the link which must exist between the wrongful act and the injury, including 'remoteness', 'directness', 'foreseeability', 'proximity', or 'intent'.[169] The ILC does not express a preference for a particular legal test of causation. It limits itself to state that 'the requirement of a causal link is not necessarily the same in relation to every breach of an international obligation' and that the injury should be 'the consequence of the wrongful act, but without the addition of any particular qualifying phrase.'[170]

---

the date of the expropriation, and in *ConocoPhillips v Venezuela* no award on damages has yet been rendered. *Quiborax v Bolivia*, where the majority decided to evaluate damages as at the date of the award, was thus only the third award in many years of investment arbitration.

165 The comparison between the actual and the but-for-scenario always remains a challenge, as the new owners make their own business decisions and choices.

166 *The Islamic Republic of Iran v The United States of America*, Award of 28 December 1998, Iran–United States Claims Tribunal Cases A15(IV) and A 24, 34 Iran–USCTR 1998, 105 paras 101–103; see ILC Commentary (n 32) Article 31, para 10; see also Ripinsky and Williams, *Damages in Investment Law* (n 2) 137.

167 Article 31 of the ILC Articles on State Responsibility.

168 Article 36 para 2, ibid.

169 ILC Commentary (n 32) Article 31, para 10.

170 ILC Commentary (n 32) Article 31, para 10.

One of the elements of causation is that speculative elements are excluded from the calculation. The ILC Commentary explains that 'tribunals have been reluctant to provide compensation for claims with inherent speculative elements.'[171] In this respect, the Iran–US Claims Tribunal in an often-quoted statement held in *Amoco v Iran*, that '[o]ne of the best settled rules of the law of international responsibility of States is that no reparation for speculative or uncertain damage can be awarded.'[172]

The tribunal in *S D Myers v Canada* required a 'sufficient causal link',[173] and noted that this meant that the harm must 'not be too remote', or that the breach of the specific NAFTA provision 'must be the proximate cause of the harm'.[174] It rejected the term 'foreseeability' as used in the law of contract to limit the range of recoverability. It emphasized that the focus should be on causation, not foreseeability, as it is the case in the law of tort or delict. The tribunal also found that the debate as to whether damages are 'direct or indirect' was not appropriate. Instead, the concept of 'remoteness' should be the key.[175] The term 'proximate cause' was also used by other tribunals.[176] The tribunal in *Feldman v Mexico* decided that 'what is owed by the responding Party is the amount of loss or damage that is *adequately* connected to the breach.'[177] The requirement is the amount of loss or damage 'actually incurred'.[178]

---

171 ILC Commentary (n 32) Article 36, para 27.

172 *Amoco International Finance v Iran*, above (n 143) para 238. See also Shufeldt Claim (*United States v Guatemala*) Award of 2 November 1929, 2 RIAA, 1079, 1099; and Robert H. May (*United States v Guatemala*) Award of 16 November 1900 in Majorie Whiteman, *Damages in International Law, vol III* (Government Printing Office, Washington 1943) 1704.

173 *S D Myers v Canada*, First Partial Award of 13 November 2000, UNCITRAL, para 316; the 'sufficient causal link' was also highlighted in *Gemplus v Mexico*, ICSID Case Nos ARB(AF)/04/3 and ARB(AF)/04/4, Award, 16 June 2010, para 11.8; *Duke Energy v Ecuador*, ICSID Case No. ARB/04/19, Award, 18 August 2008, para 468; *Biwater v Tanzania*, ICSID Case No. ARB/05/22, Award, 24 July 2008, para 779; *Archer Daniels v Mexico*, ICSID Case No. ARB(AF)/04/5, Award, 21 November 2007, para 282; *Crystallex v Venezuela*, Award of 4 April 2016, ICSID Case No. ARB(AF)/11/2, para 860.

174 *S D Myers v Canada*, Second Partial Award of 21 October 2002, UNCITRAL, para 140.

175 *S D Myers v Canada*, Second Partial Award of 21 October 2002, UNCITRAL, paras 159–160.

176 *LG&E v Argentina*, Award of 25 July 2007, ICSID Case No. 02/1, para 117; *Hoffland Honey v NIOC*, Award of 26 January 1983, 2 Iran-USCTR 41. See also the discussion of the different concepts by Ripinsky and Williams, *Damages* (n 2) 138–40.

177 *Feldmann v Mexico*, Award of 16 December 2002, ICSID Case No. ARB(AF)/99/1, para 194 (emphasis added); quoted affirmatively by *LG&E v Argentina*, ibid., para 44.

178 *Feldmann v Mexico*, ibid., para 194; *LG&E v Argentina*, ibid., paras 41–45.

With respect to the necessary evidence and burden of proof for the damage caused, there seems to be growing consensus that level of certainty is different with regard to the question whether damages have been caused and the precise calculation of the amount of damages.[179] As the tribunal in *Lemire v Ukraine* put it:

> The Tribunal agrees that it is a commonly accepted standard for awarding forward looking compensation that damages must not be speculative or uncertain, but proved with reasonable certainty; the level of certainty is unlikely, however, to be the same with respect to the conclusion that damages have been caused, and the precise quantification of such damages. Once causation has been established, and it has been proven that the in bonis party has indeed suffered a loss, less certainty is required in proof of the actual amount of damages; for this latter determination Claimant only needs to provide a basis upon which the Tribunal can, with reasonable confidence, estimate the extent of the loss.[180]

In the case of more than one separate factors combined to cause damage, international practice does not support the reduction or attenuation of reparation for concurrent causes,[181] except for cases of contributory fault.[182] The responsible state is thus held responsible for all the consequences of its wrongful conduct, unless some part of the injury can be shown to be severable.[183]

The requirement of legal causation is an essential tool for avoiding under- and overcompensation. In the comparison of the 'but-for' scenario with the actual scenario it is necessary to identify the hypothetical situation in a way that appropriately reflects the situation without the breach and considers developments, such as political and economic changes, which are not connected to the breach.

---

179 See *SPP v Egypt*, Award of 20 May 1992, ICSID Case No. ARB/84/3, para 215; *Tecmed v Mexico*, Award of 29 May 2003, ICSID Case No. ARB(AF)/00/2, para 190; *Vivendi v Argentina* (Vivendi II) Award of 20 August 2007, ICSID Case No. ARB/97/3, para 8.3.16;

180 *Joseph Charles Lemire v Ukraine*, Award of 28 May 2011, ICSID Case No. ARB/06/18, para 246; see also *Gold Reserve v Venezuela*, Award of 22 September 2014, ICSID Case No. ARB(AF)/09/1, para 686; *Crystallex v Venezuela*, Award of 4 April 2016, ICSID Case No. ARB(AF)/11/2, paras 866–870.

181 ILC Commentary, above (n 32) Article 31, para 12, with reference to the jurisprudence of the ICJ in that regard and principles of national law.

182 On contributory fault, see more details below, Section E.1.

183 ILC Commentary, above (n 32) Article 31, para 13.

VII Importance of the Valuation Date

The date on which assets are valued can have a significant impact on quantum. Possible dates in investor-state arbitration are the date of the relevant act of the state or the date of the award. In addition, the date on which the damage materializes may be relevant.[184] Furthermore, it is important what kind of information can be included in the valuation, for example whether subsequent developments shall be taken into account.

In expropriation cases, the date at which the expropriation occurred or became publicly known is generally regarded as the most appropriate date.[185] This date is contained in most BITs in order to ensure that the value of the investment is not diminished by the expropriation itself or its prior announcement.[186] As this standard represents one of the conditions for a lawful expropriation, it cannot be lower, when the state violates one of the other conditions. Furthermore, compensation should be paid promptly at the time of the expropriation so that only information available at that time should be taken into account for the valuation.

On the other hand, under the law of state responsibility, the amount of compensation payable after a violation of international law shall cover any financially assessable damage and is payable 'insofar as such damage is not made good by restitution'.[187] As 'restitution' is the primary remedy after a violation of international law,[188] it seems logical that the valuation date should be the date of the award.[189]

Nevertheless, the date of the award is not always chosen as the valuation date in investor-state arbitration. One reason may be that, under national law, as discussed above, damages in contract cases, in particular under Common Law, are only recoverable as far as they were 'foreseeable' at the time of the

---

184 See, for example, *CME v Czech Republic*, Final Award on Damages of 14 March 2003, UNCITRAL, para 492.

185 As the World Bank Guidelines in 1992 noted: 'Compensation will be deemed adequate if [...] such value is determined immediately before the time at which the taking occurred or the decision to take the asset became publicly known.' World Bank, *Legal Framework*, above (n 82) 1382.

186 See the example of the BIT provision above, Section B.2.

187 Article 36 (1) and (2) ILC Article on State Responsibility. See already above, Section B.1.

188 See the ILC Commentary, above (n 32) Article 35, para 1.

189 Greorg Schwarzenberger, *International Law as Applied by International Tribunals* (Stevens and Sons 1957) 666; similarly Max Sorenson (ed), *Manual of Public International Law* (Macmillan 1968) 567; Mark Friedman and Floriane Lavaud, 'Damages Principles in Investment Arbitration' in: Trenor, *Guide to Damages*, above (n 2) 90, 101.

breach. This seems to imply that the valuation must be done as of the date of the breach. However, under the law of State responsibility restitution is the primary remedy, and limiting factors are mainly related to causation.[190]

Another reason for the setting the valuation date in the past can be that, historically, expropriations have been the subject of the vast majority of cases between states and foreign entities, the Iran–US Claims Tribunal representing the most prominent example. In most of the cases, the value of the investment decreased dramatically or even vanished entirely after the expropriation. It was thus necessary to ensure that the expropriated property immediately before or at the date of the expropriation was the point of reference for the valuation.

However, this situation has changed, and tribunals are increasingly confronted with cases in which the value of the property has not decreased, but increased after the expropriation. In such a situation, it needs to be decided whether the lower value as of the time of the expropriation or rather the higher value as of the date of the award should be decisive. The tribunal in *ADC v Hungary* was the first to decide that, in case of an unlawful expropriation, the higher value at the time of the award needs to be chosen as it represents the best substitute for restitution under the law of state responsibility.[191] Numerous tribunals followed the reasoning that the BIT standard is only applicable for lawful expropriations, but not for unlawful expropriations,[192] even if they did not find this distinction pertinent in the case at hand.[193]

The determination of the date of the expropriation or breaches of international law is particularly difficult, when the state commits a series of acts and

---

190 See the ILC Commentary and the discussion of the issue of causation, above at (n 164).

191 *ADC v Hungary*, above (n 27) para 497. It did so by an examination of the jurisprudence of the ECtHR, most importantly the case of *Papamichalopoulos v Greece* (Just Satisfaction) ECHR Series A, No. 330-B, 31 October 1995. But also the Iran–UN Claims Tribunal held in several *obiter dicta* that the distinction between lawful and unlawful expropriations was the primacy of restitution or the valuation at the date of the award, if the asset had increased in value. See *Phillips Petroleum v Iran*, Award of 29 June 1989, 21 Iran–USCTR 79, para 110; *Amoco International Finance v Iran*, above (n 143) para 18.

192 See, for example, *Siemens v Argentina*, Award of 6 February 2007, ICSID Case No. ARB/02/8, para 353; *Vivendi v Argentina* (*Vivendi II*) Award of 20 August 2007, ICSID Case No. ARB/97/3, paras 8.2.4–6, 8.3.20; *Saipem v Bangladesh*, above (n 19) para 201; *Kardassopoulos v Georgia*, Award of 3 March 2010, para 514; *Quiborax v Bolivia*, above (n 129) para 385.

193 See, for example, *Funnekotter v Zimbabwe*, Award of 22 April 2009, ICSID Case No. ARB/05/6, para 112; *Unglaube v Costa Rica*, Award of 16 May 2012, ICSID Case No. ARB/09/20, paras 306–307.

omissions which, in their totality, caused the damage. For such indirect expropriations or other composite acts, the law of state responsibility provides that the breach occurs 'when the action or omission occurs which, taken with the other actions or omissions, is sufficient to constitute the wrongful act.'[194] Such a determination is always difficult and needs to be decided by diligent consideration of the facts. Even if this date is not the valuation date, it is still decisive for establishing the 'but for' scenario necessary to achieve full reparation and, in expropriation cases, the value of the asset at the time of the taking in order to compare the two values.

VIII The Application of Valuation Methods

Value means different things to different people. Valuation experts emphasize that it is necessary, at the beginning of every valuation, to define the 'basis' of the valuation, in other words 'value to whom?' and 'under what circumstances?'[195] The basis of the valuation describes the fundamental assumptions on which the reported value will be based.[196]

In investment arbitration, the basis of the valuation needs to be defined by the tribunal. It must clarify the premises and circumstances under which the valuation shall be carried out. The legal rules applicable and the evidence available shall inform the respective choices. In practice, tribunals often rely on the submissions of the parties, in particular if they agree on certain points. Tribunals need, however, to develop their own understanding of the basis of the valuation in order to ensure that they are in accordance with the legal rules applicable.

According to the above-mentioned valuation rules in IIAs on expropriation, the valuation should be performed on the basis of the 'fair market value' which means that the price upon which a hypothetical willing buyer and a hypothetical willing seller would agree is decisive. Conversely, the principle of 'full reparation' requires that the injured party is put in the financial position he or she would be in if the unlawful act had not been committed. In valuation practice, also a distinction can be made between valuations made under the premises

194 Article 15 (1) of the ILC Articles on State Responsibility. See Michael Reisman and Robert Sloane, 'Indirect Expropriation and its Valuation in the BIT Generation' (2003) 75 *BYIL* 115, 140 et seq.

195 Pratt and Niculita, *Valuing a Business*, above (n 100) 41.

196 IVS 2013, above (n 85).

of *value in exchange* and *value to the holder*.[197] For both premises of value, various methods of valuation are available. In the following, the three valuation approaches most widely used in business valuation and in investment arbitration shall be presented briefly.[198]

1 *Market Approach*

The market or sales comparison approach provides an indication of value by comparing the subject asset with identical or similar assets for which price information is available.[199] In general, an asset being valued is compared with sales of similar properties that have been transacted in the market. Listings and offerings may also be considered as a source of information.[200]

A variant of the market approach is the reliance on share prices of publicly traded companies.[201] The price of the stock seems to be the most reliable and objective indicator of value when the buyers and sellers are well-informed (for example, due to disclosure laws) and have no special motivation or compulsion to buy or sell.[202] Nevertheless, the company's stock prices do not necessarily reflect the value of an investment. Discounts and premiums have to be considered depending, in particular, on the number of shares (minority/control) and (lack of) marketability.[203] Furthermore, the prices of publicly traded stock are frequently rather volatile, reflecting not always purely economic but also political and psychological motives. Yet, as it is the purpose of the stock to balance supply and demand and to facilitate transactions of company shares on a market value basis, stock prices are still considered as an important yardstick.[204]

---

197 This distinction is recognized and generally accepted, as pointed out by Jay Fishman, Shannon Pratt, and William Morrison, *Standards of Value* (2nd edn, Wiley 2013) 20–1.

198 References will be made to the International Valuation Standards, one of the most authoritative standards published by the International Valuation Standards Council (IVSC) the IVS 2013, above (n 85).

199 See 'IVS Framework', in IVS 2013 (n 85) 24.

200 Ibid.

201 Ibid., 44.

202 Pratt and Niculita, *Valuing a Business*, above (n 100) 264.

203 Shannon Pratt and Alina Niculita, *The Lawyer's Business Valuation Handbook* (2nd edn, ABA 2013) (hereafter Pratt and Niculita, *Lawyer's Valuation Handbook*).

204 Kantor, *Valuation* (n 2) 15; Simon de Quidt and Phil Rees, 'Methods of Valuation: Which Method for Which Case?' in Bjorklund and others, *Current Issues* (n 2) 74; Ripinsky and Williams, *Damages in Investment Law* (n 2) 213.

Another variation of the market approach is the comparable companies method.[205] Prior transactions of similar companies are used as a benchmark. As companies are often quite dissimilar and difficult to compare, a simplified and more practical form is the use of multiples. Multiples are a particular variable of the company's performance, such as cash flow, earnings, profits, EBIT, or EBITDA, which are then multiplied by an appropriate factor.[206] Multiples are derived from sales of companies and regularly published for specific types of enterprises and industries. While multiples are relatively easy to use and intuitive, they require special expertise to assess the comparability and are still easy to misuse.[207] Tribunals have applied them usually in combination with other valuation methods.[208]

2 *Income Approach*

The income approach reflects best the prevailing opinion that the value of an asset is represented by its ability to yield financial benefits to its owner.[209] This is true for entire businesses, but also for shares in businesses, immovable property, and intangible assets, such as rents and annuities. The income approach provides an indication of value by converting expected future cash flows to a single current capital value.[210]

The most prominent of the different methodologies to arrive at the present value of future benefits is the discounted cash flow (DCF) method, because

205 The IVS refer to 'prior transactions or offers for any component of the business' as indicative of value under the market approach. See IVS 200 Businesses and Business Interests, in IVS 2013 (n 85) 43.

206 Aswath Damodaran, *Investment Valuation: Tools and Techniques for Determining the Value of Any Asset* (3rd edn, Wiley 2012) 453 (hereafter Damodaran, *Investment Valuation*); Pratt and Niculita, *Valuing a Business* (n 100) 203 et seq. EBIDTA was used to cross check the findings of the DCF valuation in *Lemire v Ukraine*, above (n 28) para 225; see also *OI European Group v Venezuela*, Award of 10 March 2015, ICSID Case No. ARB/11/25, paras 857–879.

207 Damodaran, ibid.

208 See, for example, *Crystallex v Venezuela*, Award of 4 April 2016, ICSID Case No. ARB(AF)/11/2, paras 901–905.

209 Damodaran, *Investment Valuation*, above (n 206) 1; Pratt and Niculita, *Valuing a Business*, above (n 100) 56; Tim Koller, Marc Goedhart, and David Wessels, *Valuation: Measuring and Managing the Value of Companies* (6th edn, Wiley & Sons 2015) 103 (hereafter Koller and others, *Valuation*).

210 See 'IVS Framework', in IVS 2013 (n 85) 58.

in modern valuation practices cash flow is preferred to other parameters of income, such as profits or earnings.[211]

The forecast of future cash flows requires the collection of extensive information and, based on such information, an analysis of the asset's past, present, and future situation. The forecast needs to be checked for plausibility in order to determine its reasonableness and lack of contradiction. It includes an analysis of the company's share in the respective market, general and industry-specific economic conditions, the production, finance, and competition relations and their development in the future. Both negative and positive factors must be included.

The determination of an appropriate discount rate should reflect (1) the time value of money and (2) the risk connected to the expected cash flow. The most prominently employed discount rate it the Weighted Average Cost of Capital (WACC) which is based on the Capital Asset Pricing Model (CAPM). Under this model, risk is approached from two different angles: diversifiable and non-diversifiable risk. The first type of risk is the market risk, which any enterprise operating in that particular market has to face. It can be determined on the basis of how market participants in general estimate it. The second type of risk is the non-diversifiable risk which only affecting the particular company. This type of risk is specific to the company and should not be reflected in the discount rate, but in the cash flow projection.[212]

In investor-state arbitration, the income approach has long been regarded with skepticism which was mainly based on its inherent 'speculation' about the future.[213] However, more recent tribunals apply it on a regular basis.[214] The main reason for this increased acceptance was the fact that this valuation approach has been widely used in economic practice. Tribunals could not ignore this reality any longer. Nevertheless, the complexity of the approach, most importantly the estimation of future cash flows and the risk involved, raises numerous questions in the details so that the appropriate application in

211 Damodaran, *Investment Valuation* (n 206) 6; Pratt and Niculita, *Valuing a Business* (n 100) 56.

212 Koller, Goedhart, and Wessels, *Valuation*, above (n 209) 626.

213 The Iran–US Claims Tribunal paved the way for it in *Starrett Housing* (1987) and *Phillips Petroleum* (1989). Under the auspices of ICSID, the award in *Amco v Indonesia* (*Amco II* 1990) was the first to discuss it in detail and to apply it.

214 Recent ICSID arbitrations have predominantly applied the income approach, in most cases the DCF method. See the 2017 survey and discussion by Giacchino and Sturma, 'Trends in ICSID Awards', above (n 8) 75.

a particular case will remain a challenge. A tendency can be observed to combine and cross-check the income approach with other approaches.[215]

3 *Asset-based or Cost Approach*

According to the asset value or cost approach, the value of different component parts determines the overall value of an object. The basic concept of the asset-based approach is that, if all assets and liabilities are revalued to current values, the difference between the assets and the liabilities should equal the value of the object.[216]

The advantage of this approach is that, in comparison with the income capitalization approach, it appears to be a lot easier and less speculative. It looks into the past and not into the future and is seemingly much simpler to apply than the highly complex forecasting and discounting processes. Evidence is usually available and no prognoses about the future are required. The disadvantage of this valuation approach is, however, that the value of several assets, such as certain intangible assets and goodwill, is not appropriately reflected. Furthermore, the asset-based approach does not consider the combination of the assets, and thus the value of the entity as a whole.

Investment tribunals have applied the cost approach when the prospects for the future were too uncertain to allow a meaningful cash flow forecast.[217] They have also applied it in the absence of a record of past performance.[218] While in economic practice the cost approach is hardly used and not recommended, it is still useful in investment arbitration. Costs and expenses incurred may represent the starting point for the assessment of damage caused by a BIT violation. They can also be understood as the lower limit of the amount to be compensated. Tribunals used them to evaluate the plausibility of the investor's claim for damages. In addition, costs and expenses may represent an acceptable approximation of the damage suffered, if—in the interest of a rational use of time and costs in the arbitral procedure—the employment of expensive expert valuation services were to be avoided.

215 See, for example, *National Grid v Argentina* (2008) *Gold Reserve v Venezuela* (2014) and *Crystallex v Venezuela* (2016).

216 See 'IVS Framework', in IVS 2013 (n 85) 25.

217 *Asian Agricultural Products v Sri Lanka*, Award of 27 June 1990, ICSID Case No. ARB/87/3, para 98; *Siemens v Argentina*, Award of 6 February 2007, ICSID Case No. ARB/02/8, para 355.

218 *Wena Hotels v Egypt*, Award of 8 December 2000, ICSID Case No. ARB/98/4, para 122; *Meerapfel v CAR*, Award of 21 May 2011, ICSID Case No. ARB/07/10, para 385; *Impregilo v Argentina*, Award of 21 June 2011, ICSID Case No. ARB/07/17 para 381.

4 *Mixed Approaches*

In view of the difficulties of each of the above-mentioned core methods of valuation tribunals have sometimes tried to combine them in one way or the other. The classical approach was to combine the asset based approach with the income approach. It stems from the dichotomy of *damnum emergens* and *lucrum cessans* developed under Roman law and widely recognized in contract law.[219] Under this approach, fixed assets are evaluated by their costs or replacement value and combined with some valuation of the investment's future prospects. The model example for this is *LIAMCO v Libya*, where the arbitrator first determined the asset value on the basis of book value and then added a lump sum in order to reflect the 'risks taken by LIAMCO in their pioneer works and subsequent activities'.[220] Similarly, the tribunal in *Aminoil v Kuwait* started by valuing the 'fixed assets' by a 'depreciated replacement value' and then awarded a lump sum which should also reflect the loss of 'non-fixed assets' and 'the legitimate expectations of the concessionaire'.[221]

However, this combination has been criticised as economically not sound and not in accordance with the legal principles applicable in investment arbitration.[222] The main problem is that it combines two different perspectives on value which are logically distinct. According to the prevailing opinion in valuation practice, the asset-based approach should be applied, if at all, only for an asset that has very uncertain or no future prospects.[223] The income approach should be used for all assets with future prospects.[224] The two approaches should thus be applied in the alternative, but not in combination.

---

219 See, for example, Article 7.4.2 (1) UNIDROIT Principles of International Commercial Contracts (2016): 'The aggrieved party is entitled to full compensation for harm sustained as a result of the non-performance. Such harm includes both any loss which it suffered and any gain of which it was deprived, taking into account any gain to the aggrieved party resulting from its avoidance of cost or harm.'

220 *LIAMCO v Libya*, Award of 12 April 1977, (1982) 62 ILR 141, 211–214.

221 *Aminoil v Kuwait*, Award of 24 March 1982, (1982) 21 ILM 976, para 178.

222 Sergey Ripinsky, '*Damnum Emergens* and *Lucrum Cessans* in Investment Arbitration: Entering through the Back Door' in Bjorklund and others (eds), *Investment Treaty Law*, above (n 2) 47, 60: Wöss and others, *Long-term Contracts*, above (n 2) 208–211. See also the discussion on the combination of the two approaches in *Siemens v Argentina*, Award of 6 February 2007, para. 355.

223 For example, for a start-up ventures. See 'IVS Framework', in IVS 2013, above (n 85) 25.

224 See 'IVS Framework', in IVS 2013, above (n 85) 58.

Nevertheless, the combination is still used in recent investment arbitration cases.[225]

The different valuation approaches may also be combined in another way, namely to compare and control the outcome of one valuation with the result of another. In the more sophisticated discussions of the damages issue in recent years, tribunals have been increasingly confronted with expert reports based on different approaches and combinations. Most frequently, variations of the market approach and the income approach have been presented as possible alternatives. The tribunal in *Crystallex v Venezuela* has considered four different valuation methods put forward by the claimants: (1) the stock market approach, (2) the net asset value (NAV) method, (3) the market multiples method, and (4) the indirect sales comparison method.[226] It explicitly excluded the cost approach, because it would not reflect the fair market value of the investment at the time of the expropriation.[227] After carefully considering the four methods and their outcome, the tribunal concluded that it considered the stock market and market multiples approaches as the most reliable bases upon which to value the claimant's loss.[228] It noted that the two approaches lead to results which are largely consistent with each other and decided to award the average of the two figures.[229]

The tribunal in *Rusoro v Venezuela* considered six different approaches for the valuation of the investment: (1) the amount invested, at historic prices, (2) the adjusted investment valuation, in accordance with the evolution of gold producing companies, (3) the book value of the investment, (4) the maximum market capitalization (in 2008), (5) the final market capitalization (in 2011, the expropriation date) and (6) the weighted average of three different methods as presented by the claimant's expert (comparable publicly traded

225 *Pey Casado v Chile*, Award of 8 May 2008, paras 680–683; *Duke Energy v Ecuador*, Award of 18 August 2008, para. 444; *Alpha Projektholding v Ukraine*, Award of 8 November 2010, para. 513; *Micula v Romania*, Award of 11 December 2013, paras 1238 et seq (the tribunal awarded the full amount of direct damages for increased costs, and also accepted lost profits due to higher costs for raw material); *Lahoud v DRC*, Award of 7 February 2014, paras 573 et seq.

226 *Crystallex v Venezuela*, Award of 4 April 2016, ICSID Case No. ARB(AF)/11/2, para 887.

227 Ibid., para 882.

228 Ibid., para 916.

229 The stock market approach led to an amount of US$ 1,295.17 million, the market multiples approach to an amount of US$ 1,109 million, so that the average was US$ 1,202 million. Ibid., para 917.

companies; comparable transaction; DCF valuation).[230] The tribunal rejected the income approach (DCF valuation) entirely, because it found that the circumstances in the case at hand did not allow it.[231] It also found that the final market valuation at the date of the expropriation was deeply contaminated by the respondent's policy decisions affecting the gold sector, including increased export restrictions.[232] The tribunal found that the best approach was a weighted combination of the remaining three valuations: it weighted the maximum market valuation at 25 percent, the book valuation at 25 percent, and the adjusted investment valuation at 50 percent.[233] It therefore combined the market approach with the cost-based approach, putting more emphasis on the (adjusted) cost-based approach than on the market approach.

These recent trends of tribunals to combine more approaches show a diligent discussion of the different advantages and disadvantages of various methods and throw light on the considerations of the tribunals. The result is a better understanding of the way in which a particular amount was reached and how the tribunal exercised its discretion in the determination of damages. This is particularly important when the amount is high, as it was the case in several recent awards. It does not necessarily help for a better predictability in the future, but may contribute to an increasingly better understanding of the dynamics of investment arbitration in the area of damages.

IX Opinions on Country Risk

The general economic situation in a country certainly has a major influence on the value of an investment. However, to what extent should it influence the calculation of compensation or damages in investment arbitration where the behaviour of the same countries' authorities is at issue? Should the 'country risk' be used to reduce the damage the same country has to pay to a successful claimant? While IIAs are concluded to protect investors from political risk,

230 *Rusoro v Venezuela*, Award of 13 September 2016, ICSID Case No. ARB(AF)/12/5, paras 762–770.

231 The tribunal elaborated six criteria that should, at least in significant part, be fulfilled for a meaningful application of the DCF method. Ibid., para 759. See already above, section H (b).

232 Ibid., para 779.

233 Ibid., para 789. The final award amounted to US$ 966.5 million.

they are 'not insurance policies' against bad business decisions and fluctuations in the economy.[234]

The 'country risk' can be included in the valuation of international investment, in particular when forward looking valuation methods are applied.[235] It can be evaluated on the basis of the country's US dollar sovereign debt over the US dollar risk-free rate or the relative standard deviation in stock prices,[236] or it can be reflected by diminished cash flow projections.[237] All of these methods should take account of the risk associated with investing in a particular economy, most importantly in developing or emerging countries.

The state by its decisions and actions has an important influence on the economic situation of a country and thus on the value of foreign investments. It is important to analyse what extent the country risk should be factored in the calculation of compensation and damages. While this problem has already been pertinent in the cases against Iran following the Islamic Revolution in 1979, the discussion was revived in the wake of the 'Bolivarian Revolution' by Hugo Chavez' which entailed the nationalization of companies involved in the exploitation of natural resources[238] Should the fact that this policy was proclaimed and gradually implemented be a reason for diminished amounts owed to foreign investors?

From the case law so far it can be concluded that a reduction for country risk was disallowed, when the state acted wrongfully and violated its obligations contained in the applicable IIA, most importantly the obligation to fair and equitable treatment.[239] By contrast, a reduction was allowed, when the state acted in accordance with its national and international obligations and

234 *EDF v Romania*, Award of 9 October 2009, ICSID Case No. ARB/05/13; para 217; *CMS v Argentina*, Award of 12 May 2005, ICSID Case No. ARB/01/8, para 244; *Tidewater v Venezuela*, above (n 129) paras 182–190.

235 As to the different valuation methods see further below, Section F.

236 Koller and others, *Valuation*, above (n 209) 729; Damodaran, *Investment Valuation*, above (n 206) 167–177.

237 Koller and others, *Valuation*, above (n 209) 721.

238 See the discussion of relevant cases by Florin Dorobantu, Natasha Dupont and Alexis Maniatis, 'Country Risk and Damages in Investment Arbitration' 31 ICSID Review (2015) 219; see also Markus Burgstaller and Jonathan Ketcheson, 'Should Expropriation Risk Be Taken Into Account in the Assessment of Damages' 32 ICSID Review (2016) 193.

239 *Gold Reserve v Venezuela*, Award of 22 September 2014, ICSID Case No. ARB(AF)/09/1, para 615; *OI European Group v Venezuela*, Award of 10 March 2015, ICSID Case No. ARB/11/25, para 781.

compensation for a lawful expropriation needed to be quantified.[240] In such cases, the country risk was a factor that had to be included in the quantification and resulted in a reduction of the amount that would have been payable otherwise.

X Other Possible Limitations on Damages

The obligation of a state to provide full reparation after a violation of a treaty obligation might be limited under certain circumstances.[241] In the following contributory negligence, mitigation of damages and economic emergency shall be discussed.

1 *Contributory Negligence*

Contributory negligence can reduce the duty to compensate for the damage caused by an unlawful act. The question of contribution may be regarded from different perspectives. It can be regarded as a matter of causation and thus preclude the establishment of liability,[242] or it can be seen as a matter of quantification. It can even be regarded as a matter precluding jurisdiction.[243] The ILC Articles on State Responsibility provide that contributory negligence should be regarded as a matter of quantification and stipulate in Article 39:

240 *Tidewater v Venezuela*, above (n 129) paras 182–190; *Mobil Cerro Negro v Venezuela*, Award of 4 April 2016, ICSID Case No. ARB/07/27, para 365.

241 See Borzu Sabahi, Kabir Duggal, and Nicholas Birch, 'Limits on Compensation for Internationally Wrongful Acts' in Marc Bungenberg, Jörn Griebel, Stephan Hobe, and August Reinisch (eds), *International Investment Law. A Handbook* (Beck-Hart-Nomos 2015) 1115 (hereafter Sabahi and others, 'Limits on Compensation'); Craig Miles and David Weiss, 'Overview of Principles Reducing Damages' in Trenor, *Guide to Damages*, 78 (hereafter Miles and Weiss, 'Reducing Damages').

242 In *Lauder v Czech Republic*, the tribunal found that the claimant had contributed to the destruction of its business by choosing an unreliable local partner, which was his own fault and not that of the respondent. The latter was thus not found to be liable. See *Lauder v Czech Republic*, Award of 3 September 2001, paras 234–235, 313.

243 This is comparable to the principle of 'clean hands' advanced by respondents in investment arbitration cases, see, for example, the arguments put forward by the Russian Federation in the Yukos cases. See *Yukos v Russia*, Award of 18 July 2014, PCA Case No. AA 227, paras 1273–1374.

> In the determination of reparation, account shall be taken of the contribution to the injury by wilful or negligent action or omission of the injured State or any person or entity in relation to whom reparation is sought.

A distinction can be drawn between contributory negligence unrelated to the unlawful conduct of the state, such as unwise business decisions,[244] and behavior that provoked state action.[245] Nevertheless, both cases lead to a reduction of the amount of damages. A mere contribution to the damage is, however, not sufficient; the action or omission must represent negligent and reproachable behaviour.[246] Arbitral practice seems to apply this criterion rather restrictively.[247]

As regards the extent of reduction, in the few cases in which contributory fault has been accepted the rather sweeping way this reduction was assessed[248] raised some criticism.[249] An improvement in the assessment of the extent of contributory negligence could be to relate it more closely to the issue of causation.

244 See, for example, *MTD Equity v Chile*, Award of 25 May 2004, ICSID Case No. ARB/01/7, para 242, where the tribunal criticized the unwise business decision by the investor; and *Iurii Bogdanov, Agurdino-Invest Ltd and Agurdino-Chimia JSC v Moldova*, SCC Award (22 September 2005) in which the fault was not sufficiently precisely drafting a contract. See *Yukos v Russia*, Award of 18 July 2014, para 1604.

245 See, for example, *Antoine Goetz and others v Burundi*, ICSID Case No. ARB/ 01/2, Award of 21 June 2012; and *Occidental v Ecuador*, Award of 5 October 2012, ICSID Case No. ARB/06/11, paras 662–687, where the claimants had not informed Ecuador timeously about the nature of the 'Farmount Agreement' that purported to transfer rights to a third party without obtaining ministerial authorization. See *Yukos v Russia*, Award of 18 July 2014, para 1604.

246 Brigitte Bollecker-Stern, *Le préjudice dans la théorie de la responsabilité internationale* (Pédone 1973) 195.

247 *SPP (Middle East) Ltd, Southern Pacific Properties Limited v Egypt*, ICC Award of 11 March 1983 (1983) 22 ILM 752, para 66; *CME v Czech Republic*, Final Award on Damages of 14 March 2003, UNCITRAL, paras 310 et seq.

248 In *MTD Equity v Chile* it was a 50 per cent reduction of the amount, in *Occidental Petroleum v Ecuador* and in *Yukos v Russia* it was 50 per cent.

249 Borzu Sabahi and Kabir Duggal, 'Occidental Petroleum v Ecuador (2012). Observations on Proportionality, Assessment of Damages and Contributory Fault' 28 ICSID Review (2013) 279, 288–9.

2 *Mitigation of Damages*

The duty to mitigate damages is recognized as a general principle of law.[250] In contrast to contributory negligence, it arises *after* the respondent has committed the alleged unlawful act. It implies that the injured party must take reasonable steps to reduce its losses. Depending on the facts of the case it may include selling products, stopping the delivery of services, trying to renegotiate contracts, or even giving up unprofitable projects.[251] However, this principle should not be applied too strictly, as this could favour the wrongdoer in an unjust manner.[252]

In international practice, the duty to mitigate damages has primarily been applied in breach of contract cases, which were to be decided on the basis of the terms of the contract, national contract law or general principles of contract law. The Iran–US Claims Tribunal found that the duty to mitigate damages required that after the termination of the contract or its notification, no further services were to be rendered.[253] The duty to mitigate damages could also be used for not accepting lost profits on investments not yet made[254] or

250 See ILC Commentary (n 32) Article 31, para 11; Sabahi and others 'Limits on Compensation' (n 241) 1121; *Gabčikovo-Nagymaros Project (Hungary v Slovakia)* Judgment of 25 September 1997 (1997) ICJ Reports, 7; *ME Cement v Egypt*, Award of 12 April 2002, ICSID Case No. ARB/99/6, para 167; *AIG v Kazakhstan*, Award 2 October 2003, ICISD Case No. ARB/99/6, para 10.6.4(1); *CME v Czech Republic*, Final Award on Damages of 14 March 2003, UNCITRAL, para 482.

251 Wälde and Sabahi, 'Compensation, Damages, and Valuation', above (n 1) 1096; Sabahi and others, 'Limits on Compensation', above (n 241) 1122, referring to *Bridas v Turkmenistan*, Third Partial Award and Dissent of 6 September 2000, ICC Case No. 9058/ FMS/ KGA, paras 45–53, where the tribunal reduced the award by US$ 50 million due to the claimant's failure to abandon an unprofitable oilfield.

252 According to Schwarzenberger, the principles of good faith and reasonableness, or generally the *ius aequum*, are the only measure available. Georg Schwarzenberger, *International Law as Applied by International Tribunals* (Stevens and Sons 1957) 663.

253 *Seismograph Service Corporation v NIOC*, Award of 22 December 1988, 22 Iran–USCTR (1989) 3, para 115; *Petrolane Inc v Iran*, Award of 14 August 1991, 27 Iran–USCTR (1992) 64, para 54; see also George Aldrich, *The Jurisprudence of the Iran–US Claims Tribunal* (Oxford: Clarendon Press, 1996) 300 et seq.

254 *Himpurna California Energy Ltd v PT (Persero) Perusahaan Listruik Negara (PLN)* Final Award of 4 May 1999 (2000) 25 *Yearbook of Commercial Arbitration* 13, para 347. The tribunal denied those profits by reference to the principle of 'abuse of rights'. Commentators noted, however, that the principle to mitigate damages would have been more appropriate. See Mark Kantor 'The Limitations of Arbitration' 1(2) *TDM* (2004); John Gotanda, 'Recovering Lost Profits in International Disputes' 36 Georgetown Journal of International Law (2004) 61, 104 et seq.

to limit the amount of lost profits to a certain period of time under the premise that after this period the damage could have been mitigated.[255] In general, tribunals recognize the duty to mitigate damages in principle but are rather reluctant to apply it.[256]

3 *Economic Emergency*

Host states may undergo severe economic crises which may put governments under pressure to introduce regulatory or other measures in response to mitigate and overcome the difficulties. If such measures entail the violation of international or contractual obligations by the state the question of compensation for the loss may become pertinent and whether in the calculation of such compensation the economic distress of the country should be taken in to consideration. Under international law, there are several vehicles to deal with such situations. In investor-state arbitration, the state of necessity and the 'Non-Precluded Measures Provisions' (NPMs) contained in IIAs have played a relevant role.

Necessity, under the law of state responsibility, is a circumstance precluding the wrongfulness of an act of a state. A state may be justified to breach its international obligations, including those towards a foreign investor, if such a breach is 'is the only way for the State to safeguard an essential interest against a grave and imminent peril.'[257] There are several other conditions connected so this right,[258] which have to be interpreted restrictively, including that 'the State has contributed to the situation of necessity.'[259] It has long been recognized

255 See, for example, ICC Award No. 7006, reprinted in pertinent part in (1993) 18 *YCA* 58. See also Jan Paulsson, 'The Expectation Model' in Yves Derains and Richard Kreindler (eds), *Evaluation of Damages in International Arbitration* (International Chamber of Commerce 2006) 57, 75; more examples quoted by Yasuhei Taniguchi, 'The Obligation to Mitigate Damages' in ibid., at 79 et seq.

256 After some discussion, it was denied, for example, in *ME Cement v Egypt*, Award of 12 April 2002, ICSID Case No. ARB/99/6, para 167; *Amco Asia v Indonesia*, Award of 5 June 1990 (*Amco II*) ICSID Case No. ARB/81/1, paras 78, 79; see also *Southern Pacific Properties (Middle East) v Egypt*, Award of 20 May 1992, ICSID Case No. ARB/84/3, para 245.

257 See Article 25 para 1(a) of the ILC Articles on State Responsibility.

258 These include also that the act 'does not seriously impair an essential interest of the State or States towards which the obligation exists, or of the international community as a whole' and that 'the international obligation in question excludes the possibility of invoking necessity'. See Article 25 para 1 (b) and para 2 (a) of the ILC Articles on State Responsibility.

259 Article 25 para 2 (b) of the ILC Articles on State Responsibility.

that a functioning economy represents an essential interest of a state which can lead to an exemption from payment obligations.[260] As regards the consequences for a monetary award, it is remarkable that the invocation of necessity is 'without prejudice to the question of compensation for any material loss caused by the act in question'.[261] It follows that, even if the act was not wrongful, compensation could still be due.

Necessity has been widely discussed in the context of the Argentine economic crisis between 2000 and 2002 which led the Argentine Government to enact an Emergency Law[262] and a number of other measures which had detrimental consequences on foreign investors, most importantly the so-called 'pesification' of economic terms due to the abandonment of the fixed exchange rate of the Argentina peso with the US dollar. In the subsequent ICSID proceedings, tribunals and ad hoc committees in annulment proceedings have interpreted and applied the concept of necessity differently which raised concerns about the lack of uniformity and predictability of international investment arbitration.[263]

However, keeping up legal certainty and stability in time of extreme economic crisis involves complex considerations of economic nature, most importantly with respect to the question whether the measure applied was the 'only way to safeguard' the essential interest of the state. The ICSID tribunal in *CMS v Argentina*, the first to decide the damages issue, eventually denying the state of necessity, put its dilemma in the following terms:

> The question for the Tribunal is then how does one weigh the significance of a legal guarantee in the context of a collapsing economic situation. It is certainly not an option to ignore the guarantee, as the Respondent has advocated and done, and neither is it an option to disregard the economic reality which underpinned the operation of the industry.[264]

---

260 *Russian Indemnities* (*Russia v Turkey*) Award of 11 November 1912, 11 RIAA, 431.

261 Article 27 (b) of the ILC Articles on State Responsibility.

262 *Ley emergencia publica y reforma del regimen cambiario*, Law 25.561 of 6 January 2002, Boletín Oficial, 7 January 2002.

263 August Reinisch, 'Necessity in Investment Arbitration' 41 Netherlands Yearbook of International Law (2010) 137–158; Christina Binder, 'Necessity Exceptions, the Argentine Crisis and Legitimacy Concerns: or the Benefits of a Public International Law Approach to Investment Arbitration' in Tullio Treves and others (eds), *Foreign Investment, International Law and Common Concerns* (Routledge 2014) 71–85.

264 *CMS v Argentina*, Award of 12 May 2005, ICSID Case No. ARB/01/8, para 165.

The ICSID tribunal in *LG&E v Argentina* found that the measure taken by the Argentine Government was justified, but decided that the Argentine Government should have re-established the original tariff regime more readily, so that Argentina was held responsible for the violation of its obligations after the period of necessity.[265] The tribunal in *Continental Casualty v Argentina* also accepted Argentina's contention with respect to its emergency situation, but not with respect to all claims.[266]

Other ICSID tribunals and ad hoc committees emphasized that a severe economic crisis should more appropriately be taken into account by the application of so-called 'Non-Precluded Measures Provisions' (NPMS). Such a provision, for example, is contained in Article XI of the US-Argentina BIT:

> This Treaty shall not preclude the application by either Party of measures necessary for the maintenance of public order, the fulfilment of its obligations with respect to the maintenance or restoration of international peace or security, or the Protection of its own essential security interests.[267]

The difference to the invocation of necessity is that, if the conditions are met, the BIT is not violated and thus no justification for alleged 'wrongfulness' is needed. Several ICSID awards were annulled by ad hoc committees because of the allegedly wrongful interpretation and non-application of NPMS.[268] It follows that in situations of serious economic distress, host states may take measures to address the problem without automatically having to pay for the damage caused to investors.

265 *LG&E v Argentina*, Decision on Liability of 3 October 2006, ICSID Case No. ARB/02/1, para 266.

266 *Continental Casualty v Argentina*, Award of 5 September 2008, ICSID Case No. ARB/03/9, para 236.

267 Treaty between United States of America and The Argentine Republic concerning the reciprocal encouragement and protection of investment of 14 November 1991, in force since 20 October 1994.

268 *Enron v Argentina*, Decision on the Application for Annulment of 30 July 2010, ICSID Case No. ARB/01/3, paras 347–405; *Sempra v Argentina*, Decision on the Application for Annulment of 29 June 2010, ICSID Case No. ARB/02/16, paras 159–185; the ad hoc committee in *CMS v Argentina* limited itself to heavily criticizing this lack of distinction, but ultimately refrained from annulment. See *CMS v Argentina*, Decision on the Application for Annulment of 25 September 2007, ICSID Case No. ARB/01/8, paras 134–136.

XI Thresholds for Moral Damages

Since the ICSID Tribunal in *Desert Line v Yemen* awarded US$ 1 million for 'moral damages, including loss of reputation' in 2008,[269] compensation for non-material damages has been claimed relatively frequently in investment disputes. However, tribunals have so far declined to follow the example of that decision.[270] While they repeatedly have confirmed the possibility to award moral damages and their jurisdiction in principle,[271] they have put the threshold for such damages very high. This reluctance may be understandable for the difficult financial assessment of non-material damage. However, compensating distress and suffering caused by an unlawful act should not be regarded as an extraordinary remedy, in particular, if material damage cannot be established.

The entitlement to moral damages is recognized in almost all national legal systems and under the law of state responsibility. According to Article 31 of the ILC Articles on State Responsibility compensable damage 'includes any damage, whether material or moral, caused by the internationally wrongful act'.[272] The ILC Commentary explains that 'moral' damage 'includes such things as individual pain and suffering, loss of loved ones or personal affront associated

---

269 *Desert Line v Yemen*, Award of 6 February 2008, ICSID Case No. ARB/05/17, paras 289–291. This was only the second time that an investment tribunal had awarded moral damages after the tribunal in *Benvenuti & Bonfant v Congo* in 1980, which was authorized by the parties to decide *ex aequo et bono*. See *Benvenuti & Bonfant v Congo*, Award of 15 August 1980, ICSID Case No. ARB/77/2, para 4.95.

270 An exception was the award in *Al-Kharafi v Libya*, in which the Arab Investment Court decided that the claimant was entitled to compensation for damage 'it incurred as a result of the damage to its worldwide professional reputation after the Defendants' abusive cancellation of the important project that they previously approved'. See *Al-Kharafi v Libya*, Final Arbitral Award of 22 March 2013, Arab Investment Court, 369. The tribunal awarded US$ 30 million for moral damages, in addition to US$ 900 million for lost profits and opportunities. The applicable law was the Unified Agreement for the Investment of Arab Capital in the Arab States and Libyan civil law.

271 *Pey Casado v Chile*, Award of 8 May 2008, para 704; *Funnekotter v Zimbabwe*, Award of 2009, para 140; *Siag v Egypt*, Award of 1 June 2009, para 505; *Lemire v Ukraine*, Award of 28 March 2011, para 326; *Meerapfel v CAR*, Award of 21 May 2011, para 434; *Tzu Yap Shum v Peru*, Award of 7 July 2011, para 281; *Inmaris Perestroika v Ukraine*, Award of 1 March 2012, para 428; *Arif v Moldowa*, Award of 8 April 2013, para 584; *Rompetrol v Romania*, Award of 6 May 2013, para 289; *Stati v Kazakhstan*, Award of 19 December 2013, para 1786; *Lahoud v Congo*, Award of 7 February 2014, para 620; *OI European Group v Venezuela*, Award of 2015, para 905; *Quiborax v Bolivia*, Award of 16 September 2015, para 600.

272 Article 31(2) of the ILC Articles on the Responsibility of States for Internationally Wrongful Acts, UN-Doc. A/Res/56/83, Annex.

with an intrusion on one's home or private life'.[273] The United States–Germany Mixed-Claims Commission held in an often-quoted formulation in the *Lusitania* case:

> That one injured is, under the rules of international law, entitled to be compensated for an injury inflicted resulting in mental suffering, injury to his feelings, humiliation, shame, degradation, loss of social position or injury to his credit or to his reputation, there can be no doubt, and such compensation should be commensurate to the injury. Such damages are very real, and the mere fact that they are difficult to measure or estimate by money standards makes them none the less real and affords no reason why the injured person should not be compensated therefor as compensatory damages, but not as a penalty.[274]

This description of 'moral' damages does not only include mental and physical suffering by natural persons, but also damage to reputation, which can have measurable financial consequences and also incur to legal persons. These different kinds of non-material damage probably need to be distinguished more carefully.[275] With respect to investor-state arbitration, *Sabahi* has convincingly identified the following three different types of non-material damage:

(1) *Damage to personality rights of individuals.* These include 'individual pain and suffering, loss of loved ones, or personal affront associated with an intrusion on one's home or private life. This is the typical type of non-material damages that natural persons suffer. Corporations, as juridical persons, cannot suffer such damages.

---

273 See ILC Commentary, above (n 32) Article 31, para 5; Article 36, para 16.

274 Opinion in the *Lusitania* case (*United States v Germany*) Decision of the Mixed Claims Commission of 1 November 1923, 7 RIAA, 32, 40.

275 Different proposals have been made in academic writing. See, for example, Patrick Dumberry, 'Compensation for Moral Damages in Investor-State Arbitration Disputes' 27 Journal of International Arbitration (2010) 247, 248–249; Patrick Dumberry, 'Moral Damages' in Marc Bungenberg, Jörn Griebel, Stephan Hobe and August Reinisch (eds) *International Investment Law. A Handbook* (Beck-Hart-Nomos 2015) 1130, 1132; Stephan Wittich, 'Non-Material Damage and Monetary Reparation in International Law' 15 Finish Yearbook of International Law (2004) 329, 330; Stanimir Alexandrov, 'The Present and Future of Moral Damages in Investment Arbitration' in Borzu Sabahi, Nicholas Birch, Ian Laird, and José Antonio Rivas (eds), *Revolution in the International Rule of Law. Essays in Honour of Don Wallace, Jr* (Juris 2014) 515, 516–517.

(2) *Damage to reputation.* This type of damage seems to have a dual character, as it may have clear monetary consequences and hence in some cases be considered as material.

(3) *'Legal damage'.* That is the harm that results from the *ipso facto* violation of an international obligation.[276]

The first type of damages represents the typical non-material damage which can be suffered by natural persons. It is less clear, whether a legal entity can also claim such damage incurred to its organs or employees. The tribunal in *Desert Line v Yemen* 'seems to answer this question in the affirmative'.[277] However, a sound theoretical basis for awarding moral damages to a legal entity for the injury suffered by its organs or employees seems still to be lacking.[278] In inter-state disputes such a solution is generally available under the concept of 'diplomatic protection' according to which a state may bring damage incurred by its nationals through the unlawful actions or omissions of another state in front of international courts or tribunals. One prominent case in this respect is the *Diallo* case between Guinea and the DRC, in which the International Court of Justice (ICJ) awarded Guinea the amount of US$ 85,000 'for the non-material injury suffered by Mr. Diallo'.[279] In the *Arctic Sunrise* arbitration between The Netherlands and the Russian Federation, the arbitral tribunal ordered the latter to pay EUR 600,000 to the former 'as compensation for non-material damage to the Arctic 30 for their wrongful arrest, prosecution, and detention in the Russian Federation.'[280]

This problem of legitimacy does not arise with regard to the second type of non-material damage, consisting of loss of credit or reputation. They can

276 Borzu Sabahi, *Compensation and Restitution in Investor-State Arbitration* (Oxford University Press 2011) 136–137 (emphasis in original, footnotes omitted).

277 Ibid., at 139.

278 One proposal is to refer by analogy to the doctrine of state espousal based on the 'Vattelian fiction that injury to an individual is equal to the injury of the home state of the individual'. This analogy could be used to formulate a doctrine of 'corporate espousal' according to which damage to an employee of a corporation would be considered as damage to the corporation itself. See Sabahi, above (n 2) 140. It can also be argued that harassment of the executives affects the performance of the company and/or that investor-state arbitration is the only forum where the executives could (indirectly) obtain redress for the harm suffered. See Ripinsky and Williams, *Damages in Investment Law*, above (n 2) 311.

279 *Case Concerning Ahmadou Sadio Diallo (Republic of Guinea v Democratic Republic of the Congo)* Judgment of 12 June 2012, ICJ Reports 2012, 323, 345.

280 *The Arctic Sunrise Arbitration (The Netherlands v Russian Federation)* Award on Compensation of 10 July 2017, PCA Case 2014-02, para 128.

certainly be made subject of a claim for damages by a company in investor-state arbitration.

As regards the third type of non-material damage mentioned above, consisting of 'legal damage' sustained from the *ipso facto* violation of an international obligation, the question arises, whether such non-material damage can justify a separate claim for indemnification or whether the award of a tribunal deciding on liability and damages in favour of the investor is a sufficient remedy. In inter-state disputes, the injury caused to a state by a violation of international law is excluded from compensation as not 'financially assessable' and is generally the subject matter of 'satisfaction'.[281] A declaration of the wrongfulness of the act by a competent court or tribunal is one of the most common modalities of satisfaction.[282]

Tribunals seem to apply this logic of 'satisfaction' in investor-state arbitration as well. The tribunal in *Pey Casado v Chile* decided that 'the issuance of the present award, in particular because of its recognition of the rights of the claimants and of the denial of justice of which they were victims, constitutes in itself substantial and sufficient moral satisfaction'.[283] Similarly, the tribunal in *Lemire v Ukraine* decided that 'the moral aspects of [Mr Lemire's] injuries have already been compensated by the awarding of a significant amount of economic compensation'.[284]

This logic does, however, not apply, if the investor does not receive any damages because material loss could not be proven. In this case, an award of costs by which the successful claimant is completely held harmless would be an option.[285] This solution has been chosen in cases where host states rejected

281 ILC Commentary, above (n 32) Article 36, para 1. An exception represents the Rainbow Warrior case in which the arbitral tribunal 'recommended' to France to set up a fund to promote close and friendly relations between the citizens of New Zealand and France and to pay an initial amount of US$ 2 million. *In re Rainbow Warrior*, Decision of 30 April 1990, RIAA, volume XX, 215, 275.

282 Ibid., 233. The award or judgment in itself is not sufficient, it must be accompanied by an explicit declaration which is clear and self-contained. Ibid., with reference to the *Corfu Channel* case.

283 *Pey Casado v Chile*, Award of 8 May 2008, para 704 (translation from the French original).

284 *Lemire v Ukraine*, Award of 28 March 2011, para. 233; see also *Meerapfel v CAR*, Award of 21 May 2011, para 434.

285 However, this solution was not taken up, even though it was discussed in *Rompetrol v Romania*, Award of 6 May 2013, paras 289–293. Similarly, the tribunal in *Biwater Gauff v Tanzania* rejected moral damages, even though the claimant did not receive any compensation despite various violations of the applicable BIT by the respondent. *Biwater Gauff v Tanzania*, Award of 24 July 2008, para 808. Arbitrator Born rejected the view that

'frivolous' procedures by foreign investors and claimed 'moral damages' for the damage and alleged loss of reputation incurred. The tribunals in *Europe Cement v Turkey*,[286] *Cement v Cementownia 'Nowa Huta' v Turkey*,[287] *Iberdrola v Guatemala*,[288] and *Transglobal Green Energy v Panama*[289] supported the respondents' view that the claims were ill-founded and an abuse of process so that the claimants had to pay all of the costs of the arbitration and the legal costs of the respondent.

The threshold for an award of moral damages since *Desert Line v Yemen* has remained very high. Tribunals seem to agree that moral damages may only be awarded 'in exceptional circumstances',[290] one of which is physical duress which is 'malicious and, therefore, constitutive of a fault-based liability'.[291] The tribunal in *Lemire v Ukraine* elaborated these criteria further:

> [A]s a general rule, moral damages are not available to a party injured by the wrongful acts of a State, but that moral damages can be awarded in exceptional cases, provided that
> - the State's actions imply physical threat, illegal detention or other analogous situations in which the ill-treatment contravenes the norms according to which civilized nations are expected to act;
> - the State's actions cause a deterioration of health, stress, anxiety, other mental suffering such as humiliation, shame and degradation, or loss of reputation, credit and social position; and
> - both cause and effect are grave or substantial.[292]

a favourable award was sufficient reparation for moral harm. *Biwater Gauff v Tanzania*, Award of 24 July 2008, Concurring and Dissenting Opinion, paras 32–33.

286 *Europe Cement v Turkey*, Award of 13 August 2009, para 182.

287 *Cementownia 'Nowa Huta' v Turkey*, Award of 17 September 2009, para 178.

288 *Iberdrola v Guatemala*, Award of 17 August 2012, para 518.

289 *Transglobal Green Energy v Panama*, Award of 2 June 2016, para 130.

290 *Desert Line v Yemen*, Award of 6 February 2008, para 289.

291 Ibid., para 290. This criterion was taken up in *Inmaris Perestroika v Ukraine* to deny an award of moral damages. See *Inmaris Perestroika v Ukraine*, Award of 1 March 2012, para 428; see also *Stati v Kazakhstan*, Award of 19 December 2013, para 1786.

292 *Lemire v Ukraine*, Award of 28 March 2011, para 333. Several tribunals referred to these criteria later. See, for example, *Tzu Yap Shum v Peru*, Award of 7 July 2011, para. 281; *OI European Group v Venezuela*, 10 March 2015, para. 909. The tribunal in *Arif v Moldova*, by contrast, was sceptical and noted that this formulation was rather a summary of the issues in diverse cases and should not be taken as a cumulative list of criteria that must be demonstrated for an award of moral damages. *Arif v Moldova*, Award of 8 April 2013, para 590 (emphasis added). See also Alexandrov, above (n 275) 526–527.

The criteria of 'malicious' and 'constitutive of fault based liability' are surprising insofar as the responsibility of a state is generally independent from any mental element of conduct, such as intention to harm, and thus objective.[293] The reference to 'fault' and 'egregious behaviour' may imply that tribunals, in such cases, are inclined to use their discretion to award a higher amount of damages. However, this argument comes close to a punitive function of the award of damages, which is generally not available under international law and not the purpose of moral damages.[294]

The approach by the tribunal in *Arif v Moldova* is therefore preferable which emphasized that it was necessary to go back to the older *Lusitania* case which 'leaves the Tribunal with an element of discretion, but within the general framework that moral damages are an exceptional remedy'.[295] According to the tribunal in *Arif v Moldova*, the dividing line between normal and exceptional in commercial life must be determined by a precise appreciation of the facts.[296]

Concerning the quantification of damages for moral injury, the umpire in *Lusitania*, noted that 'it is manifestly impossible to compute mathematically or with any degree of accuracy or by any use of any precise formula the damages sustained,'[297] but that 'compensation must be adequate and balance as near as may be the injury suffered'.[298] He offers some guidance for the calculation, such as the amount of lost earnings and other pecuniary loss of a deceased after a fatal injury, but also 'the amount which will reasonably compensate an injured man for suffering excruciating and prolonged physical pain; and many other inquiries concerning elements universally recognized as constituting recoverable damages.'[299]

293 See ILC Commentary, above (n 32) Article 2, para 10.

294 The line between 'moral' and 'punitive' damages was blurred by the ICSID Tribunal in *Siag v Eygpt* which noted that 'the recovery of punitive or moral damages is reserved for extreme cases of egregious behavior.' *Siag v Eygpt*, Award of 1 June 2009, para. 545. See also Stephen Jagusch and Thomas Sebastian, 'Moral Damages in Investment Arbitration: Punitive Damages in Contemporary Clothing' 29 Journal of International Arbitration (2012) 45; Stephan Wittich, 'Punitive Damages', in James Crawford, Alain Pellet, and Simon Olleson (eds), *The Law of International Responsibility* (Oxford University Press 2010) 667.

295 *Arif v Moldova*, Award of 8 April 2013, para 591.

296 Ibid., para 603.

297 Opinion in the *Lusitania* case (*United States v Germany*) Decision of the Mixed Claims Commission of 1 November 1923, 7 RIAA, 32, 36.

298 Ibid.

299 Ibid.

To evaluate human pain and suffering is certainly a difficult task with which investment tribunals are not familiar with. However, they could take some guidance from jurisprudence on human rights, which quantifies damages for human rights violations on a regular basis.[300] This is what the ICJ in *Diallo* did when it awarded US$ 85,000 for moral damages to the successful claimant. In arriving at that amount, the ICJ looked at the practice of the United Nations Human Rights Committee, the African Commission on Human and People's Rights, the ECtHR, and the Inter-American Court of Human Rights.[301]

As regards compensation for damages to reputation, including loss of goodwill, creditworthiness, or even business opportunities, quantification appears to be easier, because they have an economic underpinning and can be substantiated by evidence. However, they have a dual character and can be part of a claim for material as for moral damage. As the threshold for moral damages is high, it might be possible to formulate some of those claims as material damages. The submission of sufficient evidence may also be a challenge,[302] but in a few cases tribunals have accepted them.[303]

For the quantification for mere 'legal damage', in addition to the above-mentioned solution through an award on costs, guidance may be sought again in the jurisprudence of the ECtHR. In addition to its regular practice of assessing non-material damages caused by human rights violation, the ECtHR uses moral damages also in the context of the violation of property rights which are protected under the European Convention on Human Rights.[304] It uses moral damages with respect to the distinction between lawful and unlawful expropriations:

---

300 See Ewa Baginska (ed), *Damages for Violations of Human Rights. A Comparative Study of Domestic Legal Systems* (Springer International Publishing 2016); Dinah Shelton, *Remedies in International Human Rights Law* (2nd edn, Oxford University Press 2005) 38, 343–344.

301 *Case Concerning Ahmadou Sadio Diallo (Republic of Guinea v Democratic Republic of the Congo)* Judgment of 12 June 2012, ICJ Reports 2012, 323, 334–335.

302 The ICSID tribunal *SOABI v Senegal* rejected the claim to 'general damages for loss of goodwill and loss of commercial financing' because it regarded such damage as 'wholly hypothetical'. *SOABI* v *Senegal*, Award of 25 February 1988, para 10.01; see also *Atlantic Triton v Guinea*, Award of 21 April 1986, para 3.2.

303 *Shufeldt Claim* (United States v Guatemala) Award of 2 November 1929, 2 RIAA, 1079, 1101; *Robert H May* (United States v Guatemala) Award of 16 November 1900 in Whiteman, *Damages*, above (n 172) 1704, 1709; *Funnekotter v Zimbabwe*, Award of 22 April 2009, para 137; *Swisslion v Macedonia*, Award of 6 July 2012, para. 350; see also Alexandrov, above (n 275) 518.

304 Article 1 of the First Protocol of the European Convention on Human Rights.

> The Court considers that the feelings of powerlessness and frustration arising from the unlawful dispossession of their property has caused the applicants considerable non-pecuniary damage that should be compensated in an appropriate manner. Ruling on an equitable basis, as required by Article 41 of the Convention, it decides to award EUR 15,000 to each of the applicants under this head, or EUR 45,000 in total.[305]

While this practice and statement of reasons cannot be taken up as such in investment arbitration,[306] this should not rule out the possibility that tribunals use their competence to award 'full reparation' for injury and try to assess the 'feelings of powerlessness and frustration' and also loss of reputation and business opportunities which are inherently connected to a violation of an international obligation. This could avoid situations in which the violations of provisions in IIAs do not lead to an award of damages at all, due to lack of sufficient evidence or causation for material damage.

XII Interest

Despite the importance of interest from a financial point of view, the applicable rules for their determination are still relatively underdeveloped in international investment arbitration.[307] While the length and detail of submissions

305 *Guiso-Gallisay v Italy*, ECHR 58858/ 00, Grand Chamber, Judgment of 22 December 2009 (just satisfaction) para. 102.

306 The tribunals are usually called to apply the BIT standard or the standard of full reparation according to the ILC Articles on State Responsibility, while the ECtHR has the competence to award 'just satisfaction' on the basis of Article 41 of the European Convention on Human Rights (ECHR). See the discussion above, section C.

307 Some insightful analyses and commentaries have been provided in the literature, though. See, for example, Francis A Mann, 'Compound Interest as an Item of Damages in International Law' UC Davis Law Review (1988) 577; John Gotanda, 'Awarding Interest in International Arbitration' 90 AJIL (1996) 40; John Gotanda, *Supplemental Damages in Private International Law* (Kluwer Law International 1997); Brower and Brueschke, *The Iran–US Claims Tribunal*, above (n 143) 615 et seq; John Gotanda, 'Compound Interest in International Disputes' Oxford University Comparative Law Forum (2004) 2; Jeffrey Colón and Michael Knoll, 'Prejudgment Interest in International Arbitration' 4(6) TDM (2007); Thierry Sénéchal, 'Time Value of Money: A Case Study' 4(6) TDM (2007); John Gotanda, 'A Study of Interest' Villanova University School of Law/Public Law and Legal Theory Working Paper No. 2007–10 (August 2007); Ripinsky and Williams, *Damages in Investment Law* above (n 2) 361–391; Kantor, *Valuation* above (n 2) 261–287; Thierry Sénéchal and John Gotanda, 'Interest as Damages' 47 Columbia Journal of Transnational Law (2009)

by the parties and statement of reasons by tribunals have increased in the past years, tribunals have yet to ascertain uniform principles on the selection of the appropriate interest rate, the period of interest, the issue of compounding, and whether there should be a distinction between pre-award and post-award interest.

In the following, these aspects will be briefly discussed in the light of recent arbitral practice.[308] Despite the lack of a general consensus, it seems to be appropriate to distinguish between pre-award and post-award interest, because the former represents an item of compensation or damages, while the latter functions as default charges for the non-payment of a debt.[309]

1 *Pre-award Interest*

Pre-award interest has different functions in expropriation and non-expropriation cases. In the context of expropriations of foreign property the claim to interest results from the requirement that compensation has not only to be 'adequate and effective', but must also be 'prompt'. Prompt' means 'paid without delay'.[310] In the context of calculating compensation in cases of state responsibility the duty to pay interest results from the obligation to provide 'full reparation'.[311] In both cases, tribunals need to decide on the interest rate, the day at which interest start running (*dies a quo*), and on the issue whether interest should be compounded.

491; Ripinsky and Williams, *Damages in Investment Law* above (n 2) 361–91; Elihu Lauterpacht and Penelope Nevill, 'Interest' in James Crawford, Alain Pellet, and Simon Olleson (eds), *The Law of International Responsibility* (Oxford University Press 2010) 613–22; Abdala, Zadicoff, and Spiller, 'Invalid Round Trips', above (n 116) 1–19; Mick Smith and Romans Vikis, 'Whose Money is it and Should it Matter? An Essay on the Cost of Capital in International Arbitration' 10(4) TDM (2013); Inna Uchkunova and Oleg Temnikov, 'A Procrustean Bed: Pre- and Post-Award Interest in ICSID Arbitration' 29 ICSID Review (2014) 648–68; Mark Beeley and Rory Walck, 'Approaches to the Award on Interest by Arbitration Tribunals' 1(1) Journal of Damages in International Arbitration (2014) 51–76; John Gotanda, 'Interest' in Mark Bungenberg, Jörn Griebel, Stephan Hobe, and August Reinisch (eds), *International Investment Law. A Handbook* (Beck-Hart-Nomos 2015) 1142–1153; Aaron Dolgoff and Tiago Duarte-Silva, 'Prejudgment Interest: An Economic Review of Alternative Approaches' 33 Journal of International Arbitration (2016) 99–114.

308 For a more detailed and historical analysis see Marboe, *Calculation*, above (n 2) 327–405.

309 As from the date of the award, the respondent is essentially in default of payment. See *Gold Reserve v Venezuela*, Award of 22 September 2014, para 856.

310 World Bank, *Legal Framework*, above (n 82) 1363, 1383.

311 Article 36 of the ILC Articles. See also the discussion on the standard of compensation under the law of State responsibility above, section D. b.).

a Interest Rate

IIAs generally provide that, in cases of expropriation, compensation must include interest at a rate that is 'commercial', 'commercially reasonable', 'market based' or set at 'usual bank interest'.[312] Article 1110 NAFTA refers to 'interest at a *commercially reasonable rate* for that currency from the date of expropriation until the date of actual payment'.[313] Article 13 ECT states that '[c]ompensation shall also include interest at a *commercial rate* established on a market basis from the date of Expropriation until the date of payment'.[314] Only rarely a specific market interest, such as LIBOR or EURIBOR, is mentioned.[315] Some BITS require 'fair and equitable' interest.[316]

These IIA provisions make clear that statutory interest provided under national law in the home state of the investor or the host state is not an option. However, they do not explain which rate may be regarded as a 'commercial', 'commercially reasonable', etc., rate. Should lending rates or borrowing rates be applied? Whose borrowing or landing rate should be taken, that of the claimant or that of the respondent? Are inter-bank rates appropriate, and if so, with or without an additional premium? Should the cost of capital of the investor be applied for determining pre-award interest? Or should the borrowing rate of the respondent state be decisive, because the delay actually turns the claimant into an involuntary lender?

Similar questions arise in the context of calculating compensation in cases of state responsibility. Article 38 of the ILC Articles on State Responsibility states in this respect:

> Interest on any principal sum payable under this Chapter shall be payable when necessary in order to ensure full reparation. The interest rate and mode of calculation shall be set as to achieve that result.[317]

312 See, for example, Article 6 (3) US Model BIT (2012); Article 13 (3) Canada Model BIT (2004) Article 5 (2) France Model BIT (2006); Article 4 (2) Germany Model BIT (2008); Article VI (4) Colombia Model BIT (2007).

313 Article 1110 para 3 NAFTA.

314 Article 14 paras 2 and 1(g) ECT.

315 Article V (3) Model BIT of Italy (2003) refers to 'interest calculated on the basis of EURIBOR standards'. The BIT between Brazil and Finland (1995) refers to 'interest at London Interbank Offered Rate (LIBOR).

316 Article 5 (1) India Model BIT (2003) requires 'interest at a fair and equitable rate'. See also India–UK BIT (1994); Egypt–India BIT (1997).

317 Article 38(1) Articles on the Responsibility of States for Internationally Wrongful Acts, Annex to General Assembly Resolution 56/ 83 of 12 December 2001, UN Doc A/ Res./56/ 83.

This formulation also has the consequence that statutory interest is not appropriate for determining pre-award interest, but that considerations of an economic nature are necessary. Yet, it is not clear what kind of commercial reference should be taken.

The borrowing rate of the successful claimant has gained some support in literature and arbitral practice, reflecting the assumption that the investor needed to take out a loan in his home state in order to bridge the gap caused by the delay in payment.[318] The Iran–US Claims Tribunal introduced the 'prime rate', which is the interest rate commercial banks charge their most creditworthy borrowers, as an appropriate benchmark to determine the borrowing rate of the investor.[319] The 'prime' or 'base' rate plays an important role in negotiations about company loan conditions in Anglo-American countries. However, not all enterprises can borrow money from the banks at the prime rate so that an increase by a few percentage points might be necessary. The question then arises, how many percentage points are appropriate. The practice of tribunals is not entirely consistent.

The prime rate was applied to set pre-award interest *Teco v Guatemala* with additional two percentage point premium.[320] In *Pluspetrol v Perupetrol*, the tribunal awarded the prime rate plus three percentage points.[321] No premium was added to the US or New York prime rate in *Mobil Cerro Negro v Venezuela*,[322] *Chevron v Ecuador*,[323] *Mobil Cerro Negro v PDVSA*,[324] and *Cargill v Mexico*.[325]

The prime rate in the currency of the country of the business can also be used. The tribunal in *S D Myers v Canada* was of the opinion that the borrowing rate of the investor in the host state rather than in the home state of the investor should be decisive.[326] In addition, the Canadian dollar had been

318 The 'prime. See the website of the US Board of Governors of the Federal Reserve System, <https://www.federalreserve.gov/faqs/credit_12846.htm>; see also *Sylvana Technical Systems v Iran*, 8 Iran–US CTR (1985) 298, 321 in fn 12.

319 See Arbitrator Holtzmann who argued that it 'is reasonable to assume that most businesses habitually borrow while fewer regularly invest in certificates of deposit.' *Sylvana Technical Systems Inc v Iran*, Award of 27 June 1985, Separate Opinion of Arbitrator Holtzmann, 8 Iran–US CTR (1985) 298, 321 in fn. 13.

320 *Teco v Guatemala*, Award of 19 December 2013, paras 766 et seq.

321 *Pluspetrol v Perupetro*, Award of 21 May 2015, para 207.

322 *Mobil Cerro Negro v Venezuela*, Award of 9 October 2014, para 396.

323 *Chevron v Ecuador*, Award of 31 August 2011, para 350.

324 *Mobil Cerro Negro v PDVSA*, Award of 23 December 2011, para 854.

325 *Cargill v Mexico*, Award of 18 September 2009, para 544.

326 *S D Myers v Canada*, Second Partial Award of 21 October 2002, para 305.

the currency of account so that the standard Canadian prime rate was accordingly taken as the reference rate, increased by one percentage point.[327]

Instead of an estimation or approximation of the borrowing rate of the investor, the actual borrowing rate of the investor could be used as a rate for pre-award interest. As a matter of principle, this could be an appropriate way of remedying the concrete loss incurred by the delay because he or she must finance the funds in the meantime. It is possible to estimate the cost of borrowing, for example, by averaging the different interest margins over the risk-free rate over the years or by assuming an average debt profile for the company under review.[328] One could also try to obtain the ratio of finance charges over the debt for similar firms over a period of time and take a weighted average.[329] These methods, however, depend on many assumptions and variables and on the exercise of judgement. In order to avoid an arbitrary result the tribunal must become truly acquainted with the internal structures, the risk profile, and finance practices of the company.

The tribunal in *Tidewater v Venezuela* did not find it too complicated to apply the claimants borrowing rate.[330] It noted that the claimants' expert had pointed out that the parent company of the claimants was able to borrow at rates between 4.35 per cent and 4.47 per cent during the period in question. The tribunal thus considered 'that an interest rate of 4.5% most closely meets the standard agreed between Venezuela and Barbados in Article 5 of the BIT'.[331] In support of that rate, the tribunal pointed out that the claimants had proposed in the alternative the US prime rate plus two percentage point or the LIBOR plus four percentage points. As these two averaged 5.2 per cent, the concrete borrowing rate was the lowest of these alternatives.

Some argue that the borrowing rate of the investor is in fact its cost of capital.[332] The cost of capital is an 'opportunity cost' and represents the expected rate of return that investors give up by investing in the subject investment instead of investing in an available alternative investment comparable in terms of risk and other investment characteristics.[333] The cost of capital

327 Ibid., para 307.

328 Sénéchal, 'Time Value of Money', above (n 307) 8.

329 Ibid.

330 *Tidewater v Venezuela*, above (n 129) paras 207–209.

331 Ibid., para 207.

332 Smith and Vikis, 'Whose Money', above (n 307) 5; Abdala, Zaidcoff, and Spiller, 'Invalid Roundtrips', above (n 116) 12.

333 Pratt and Niculita, *Valuing a Business*, above (n 100) 181.

is also used for discounting investment cash flows.[334] It needs to be avoided that an expected cash flow is discounted at a high rate of cost of capital and then adjusted to present value at a very low risk free rate, which represents an 'invalid round trip'.[335] However, others are skeptical, because the cost of capital represents an *ex ante* expectation involving certain risks, while pre-award interest is an *ex post* calculation of compensation only requiring time-value adjustments to an awarded damages amount known with certainty.[336] In arbitral practice, the use of the cost of capital for the determination of pre-award interest has been discussed several times,[337] but only rarely been accepted.[338]

Another estimation of the borrowing rate of the investor may be arrived at by using interbank rates. The tribunal in *National Grid v Argentina* found it realistic to assume that the claimant would have applied the sums received either to eliminate existing debts or avoid incurring additional debt.[339] However, it did not have sufficient data to apply a particular interest rate as the concrete claimant's borrowing rate. The tribunal thus reverted to the LIBOR (London Interbank Offered Rate) rate plus two percentage points as an average borrowing rate:

> In the absence of Claimant's borrowing rate in the record, the Tribunal will utilize a widely recognized conservative measure, which has been adopted in the awards of previous international arbitration tribunals, namely LIBOR plus 2%.[340]

The LIBOR, similar as the EURIBOR (European Interbank Offered Rate), represents the interest rate at which banks offer to lend funds (wholesale money) to one another in the international interbank market. The LIBOR is rated in five currencies and for seven maturities.[341] The LIBOR (and EURIBOR) are market related because they represent the basis for many loan negotiations

---

334 See above the discussion on the 'income approach' in valuation, section H b).

335 Abdala, Zadicoff, and Spiller, above, 'Invalid Roundtrips' (n 116) 12; Beeley and Walck, 'Interest', above (n 307) 76; Wöss and others, *Long-term Contracts* (supra 2) 281–286.

336 Dolgoff and Duarte-Silva, 'Prejudgment Interest', above (n 307) 102.

337 *PSEG v Turkey*, Award of 19 January 2007, paras 341–345; *EDF, SAUR and León v Argentina*, Award of 11 June 2011, para 1325; *Swisslion v Macedonia*, Award of 6 July 2012, para 358; *TECO v Guatemala*, Award of 19 December 2013, paras 762–768.

338 *Phillips Petroleum and ConocoPhillips v PDVSA*, Award of 17 September 2012, para 295.

339 *National Grid v Argentina*, Award of 3 November 2008, para 294.

340 Ibid.

341 USD, GBP, EUR, JPY, CHF; the maturities are between overnight and one year. See the website of global-rates <http://www.global-rates.com/interest-rates/libor/>.

and finance decisions. However, it is also known for its fluctuation. The six months-LIBOR for US dollars has fallen from 6.7 percent in 2000 to 0.9 percent in 2016.[342] Furthermore, it is not particularly easy to calculate, because it has to be re-assessed regularly on the basis of the indicated maturity (eg six months) over the running period of pre-award interest.[343]

Whether the LIBOR in international investment arbitration is used as a proxy of the borrowing rate of the claimant or of the state, or as a proxy to a lending rate in an 'alternative investment'-approach, is not always clear.[344] Nevertheless, it has increasingly been used by tribunals as a commercial rate, sometimes without,[345] but more frequently with the addition of several percentage points.[346] Tribunals often do not provide explanations for these additional percentage points and why they chose two, three or four. The tribunal in *Lemire v Ukraine*, as one of the exceptions, stated that it tried to get as close as possible to the claimant's borrowing rate and therefore added a

---

342 See the website of global-rates <http://www.global-rates.com/interest-rates/libor/american dollar/usd-libor-interest-rate-6-months.aspx>.

343 Beeley and Walck, 'Interest', above (n 307) 75–76.

344 The 'alternative investment'-approach assumes that pre-award interest should be based on interest the investor could have earned, if he had been paid in time and thus had funds available for an alternative investment. See *Sylvana Technical Systems v Iran*, above (n 318) 320. This approach is also advanced by John Gotanda in his early publication on interest in AJIL in 1996, see Gotanda, 'Awarding Interest in International Arbitration', above (n 307) 56.

345 *Biloune v Ghana*, Award on Damages and Costs of 30 June 1990, (1994) 95 ILR 211, 230; *Emilio Agustín Maffezini v Spain*, Award of 13 November 2000, para 96; *MTD v Chile*, Award of 25 May 2004, para 249; *Siag v Egypt*, Award of 1 July 2009, para 597; *Rosinvest v Russia*, Award of 22 September 2010, para 686. *Swisslion v Macedonia*, Award of 6 July 2012, para 358.

346 The most widely used premium is two percentage points, See, for example, *PSEG v Turkey*, Award of 19 January 2007, para 348; *Enron v Argentina*, Award of 22 May 2007, para 452; *Sempra v Argentina*, Award of 28 September 2007, para 486; *Rumeli v Kazakhstan*, Award of 28 July 2008, para 818; *Continental Casualty v Argentina*, Award of 5 September 2008, para 314; *National Grid v Argentina*, Award of 3 November 2008, para 294; *Lemire v Ukraine*, Award of 28 March 2011, para 351, see the discussion already above; *El Paso v Argentina*, Award of 31 October 2011, para 743; *Railroad Development v Guatemala*, Award of 29 June 2012, paras 278–279; *Lahoud v DRC*, Award of 7 February 2014, para 631; *Khan v Resources v Mongolia*, Award of 2 March 2015, para 425; *Quiborax v Bolivia*, above (n 129) para 517. Four percentage points were added in *Kardassopoulos and Fuchs v Georgia*, Award of 3 March 2010, para 661, and *Mobil Investments and Murphy Oil v Canada*, Award of 20 February 2015, para 170. Only one percentage point was added in *SGS v Paraguay*, Award of 2012, para 188 (US$ thirty-day LIBOR rate) and in *Crystallex v Venezuela*, Award of 4 April 2016, para 934 (six-months average US$ LIBOR rate).

premium of two percent. It held that this was a 'reasonable margin, which reflects the surcharge which an average borrower would have to pay for obtaining financing based on LIBOR'.[347]

However, the LIBOR will not remain at the disposal as an interest rate in international arbitration for long, as the UK's Financial Conduct Authority (the FCA, the UK's key financial regulator) publicly announced that the FCA would phase out LIBOR by the end of 2021.[348] This means that also in international investment arbitration this rate will no longer be available after that date. Tribunals will then have to find another commercial or market oriented rate. In so doing they might be compelled to reflect more in detail which approach is most appropriate to remedy the financial harm inflicted by the delay in payment.

b Dies a quo

It is important that the date from which interest is to accrue (*dies a quo*) is determined consistently with the other parameters of the quantification, most importantly with the valuation date. If the valuation date is the date of the award, granting pre-award interest would amount to double counting. If the valuation date lies in the past, several options for the beginning of the period of pre-award interest are possible.

In cases of expropriation, IIAs set the beginning of the interest period at the date of the expropriation.[349] As regards cases of state responsibility, '[i]nterest runs from the date when the principal sum should have been paid until the date the obligation to pay is fulfilled'.[350] This formulation leaves open, when the principal sum should have been paid so that the various options need to be explored.

One option is the date of the unlawful act, because at that time the state's international responsibility becomes engaged.[351] Another option is the date at which the damage actually occurred, because the violation of an international

347 *Lemire v Ukraine*, Award of 28 March 2011, para 356.

348 Alexander Fraser and Cheryl Aaron, 'End of LIBOR in UK: Impact on Loan Documents and Swaps', The National Law Review of 8 August 2017, see https://www.natlawreview.com/article/end-libor-uk-impact-loan-documents-and-swaps; special thanks to Mark Kantor who posted this news at the listserv Oil-Gas-Energy-Mining-Infrastructure Dispute Management (ogemid@ogeltdm.com) on 16 August 2017.

349 As regards the difficulty in determining the expropriation date in cases of indirect expropriations, see above, section G.

350 Article 38 of the ILC Articles on State Responsibility.

351 *Asian Agricultural Products v Sri Lanka*, Award of 27 June 1990, para 114; see the more recent practice in *Impregilo v Argentina*, Award of 21 June 2011, para 384; *Swisslion*

obligation may not immediately cause damage, but the obligation to pay cannot arise earlier than the damage.[352]

Again another option would be the date on which legal proceedings are initiated, based on national law provisions,[353] submissions by the parties[354] or the tribunal's discretion.[355] This seems, however, hardly compatible with the legal principles as well as with the function of interest as described above.

c Compounding

While simple interest was the prevailing practice in international arbitration and adjudication for a long time,[356] in recent years, compound interest has been increasingly accepted in investment arbitration and nowadays represent the rule rather than the exception. The arguments by some commentators reflected in arbitral proceedings paved the way for a more open attitude towards compound interest, mainly based on the reasoning that 'most financing and investment vehicles available to parties in transnational business involve compound interest.'[357]

---

v Macedonia, Award of 6 July 2912, para 359; *Lahoud v DRC*, Award of 7 February 2014, para 633.

352 See Report of the International Law Commission on the work of its fifty-second session, UN Doc. A/ 55/ 10, Supplement No. 10, 69. See, for example, *Siemens v Argentina*, Award of 6 February 2007, para 403.7; *Abengoa v Mexico*, Award of 18 April 2013, para 784; *Micula v Romania*, Award of 11 December 2013, para 1329; *Suez v Argentina*, Award of 19 April 2015, para 105.

353 *Amco Asia v Indonesia (Amco I)* Award of 20 November 1984, para 239; *Marvin Feldman v Mexico*, Award of 16 December 2002, para 205; *CME v Czech Republic*, Final Award on Damages of 14 March 2003, paras 631 et seq.

354 *Atlantic Triton v Guinea*, Award of 21 April 1986 (1995) 3 ICSID Reports 13, 30; *Pope & Talbot v Canada*, Award in Respect of Damages of 31 May 2002, para 90.

355 *Asian Agricultural Products v Sri Lanka*, Award of 27 June 1990, para 115; *S D Myers v Canada*, Second Partial Award of 21 October 2002, para 303.

356 See the often-quoted statement by Majorie Whiteman: 'There are few rules within the scope of the subject of damages in international law that are better settled than the one that compound interest is not allowable.' Whiteman, *Damages*, above (n 172) 1997.

357 Gotanda, 'Compound Interest', above (n 307), text after fn 324; earlier, F A Mann published his arguments in favour of compound interest in F A Mann, 'Compound Interest as an Item of Damages in International Law' UC Davis Law Review (1988) 540–585, 577; see also the critique of the practice of the Iran-US Claims Tribunal in this respect by Brower and Brueschke, *Iran–US Claims Tribunal*, above (n 143) 629–630.

The trend in investment arbitration started to change in the year 2000, when a number of ICSID tribunals awarded compound instead of simple interest.[358] It seemed to be increasingly accepted that 'compound interest would better compensate the Claimants for the actual damages suffered since it better reflects contemporary financial practice.'[359] The tribunal in *Lemire v Ukraine* explained that 'an unpaid lender has to resort to the LIBOR market, in order to fund the amounts due but defaulted, and the lender's additional funding costs have to be covered by the defaulting borrower'.[360] Other considerations, such as the length and conduct of the parties in the proceedings, only rarely played a role.[361]

The compounding intervals of pre-award interest varied between compounded annually[362] or semi-annually.[363] A few tribunals compounded

358 *Compañía del Desarrollo de Santa Elena v Costa Rica*, Award of 17 February 2000, para 104; *Metalclad Corp v Mexico*, Award of 30 August 2000, para 128; *Emilio Agustín Maffezini v Spain*, Award of 13 November 2000, para 277; *Wena Hotels v Egypt*, Award of 8 December 2000, para 129.

359 *LG&E v Argentina*, Award of 25 July 2007, para 103.

360 *Lemire v Ukraine*, Award of 28 March 2011, para 360.

361 The tribunal in *Railroad Development v Guatemala* referred to the 'length of these proceedings because of two jurisdictional phases in which the jurisdictional objections of Respondent were rejected, and several postponements in the procedural calendar at the Government's request.' *Railroad Development v Guatemala*, Award of 29 June 2012, para 281.

362 *Impregilo v Argentina*, Award of 21 June 2011, para 383; *EDF, SAUR and León v Argentina*, Award of 11 June 2012, disposition no. III; *Goetz v Burundi*, Award of 21 June 2012, para 307; *Quasar de Valores*, Award of 20 July 2012, para 228; Occidental v Ecuador, Award of 5 October 2012, para 845; TECO v Guatemala, Award of 19 December 2013, paras 766–767; SAUR v Argentina, Award of 22 May 2014, para 433; *Gold Reserve v Venezuela*, Award of 22 September 2014, para 855; *Mobil Cerro Negro v Venezuela*, Award of 9 October 2014, para 399; *Flughafen Zürich v Venezuela*, Award of 18 November 2014, para 962; *Khan Resources v Mongolia*, Award of 2 March 2015, para 425; *OI European Group v Venezuela*, Award of 10 March 2015, para 953; *Quiborax v Bolivia*, above (n 129) paras 520–521; *Crystallex v Venezuela*, Award of 4 April 2016, para 940.

363 *Lemire v Ukraine*, Award of 28 March 2011, paras 357 et seq; *Tza Yap Shum v Peru*, Award of 7 July 2011, para 291; *El Paso v Argentina*, Award of 31 October 2011, para 746; *Unglaube v Costa Rica*, Award of 16 May 2012, para 324; *Swisslion v Macedonia*, Award of 6 July 2012, para 358; *Anatolie and Gabriel Stati v Kazakhstan*, Award of 18 December 2013, para 1855; *Hassan Awdi v Romania*, Award of 2 March 2015, para 519; *Suez v Argentina*, Award of 9 April 2015, para 117; *Hrvatska Elektroprivreda v Slovenia*, Award of 17 December 2015, paras 559–560; *Tenaris v Venzuela*, Award of 29 January 2016, para 594.

quarterly,[364] some others monthly.[365] It happened also that no compounding interval was indicated.[366] It is important that benchmark rates and the compounding intervals match so that, for example, interest based on six-month US certificate of deposit is compounded semi-annually, and not annually.[367]

Despite this increasing consensus, simple interest also has been awarded in some investment arbitration cases even after the year 2000. The tribunal in *Autopista Concesionada v Venezuela* analysed whether compound interest should be awarded on the basis of an agreement by the parties, or according to national law or international law.[368] Emphasizing that the case dealt with a breach of contract and not with expropriation it held that 'there is a tendency in international jurisprudence to award only simple interest [...] in relation to breach of contract'.[369] This was subsequently taken up by other tribunals dealing with breaches of contracts.[370] Yet, a few expropriation cases did not lead to an award of compound interest, either.[371]

Another line of cases with simple interest concerned arbitral awards which had not been enforced by the respondent state and which had not included an award of interest in the first place.[372] In some cases, the high amount of the principal seems to raise reluctance on the part of the tribunal to increase it by an amount of compound interest.[373] The tribunal in *Yukos v Russia* found, after awarding US$ 50 billion as principal, that 'in the circumstances of this case, it

---

364 *Micula v Romania*, Award of 11 December 2013, para 1272; *Tidewater v Venezuela*, above (n 129) para 209.

365 *Mobil Investments v Canada*, Award of 20 February 2015, para 170.

366 *LG&E v Argentina*, Award of 25 July 2007, paras 103, 115; *Railroad Development v Guatemala*, Award of 29 June 2012, para 281.

367 See Beeley and Walck, above (n 307) 62, referring to *Siemens v Argentina*, in which a rate based on six-month US certificates of deposit was compounded annually, not semi-annually. See *Siemens v Argentina*, Award of 6 February 2007, paras 396–400; see also Gotanda, 'A Study of Interest', above (n 307) 25.

368 *Autopista Concesionada de Venezuela v Venezuela*, Award of 23 September 2003, paras 394 et seq.

369 Ibid., para 394.

370 *Duke Energy v Ecuador*, Award of 18 August 2008, para 457; *Pluspetrol v Perupetro*, Award of 21 May 2015, para 207.

371 *Abengoa v Mexico*, Award of 18 April 2013, para 787; *Lahoud v DRC*, Award of 7 February 2014, para 632.

372 *Desert Line v Yemen*, Award of 6 February 2008, para 298; *Saipem v Bangladesh*, above (n 19) para 211.

373 In *CME v Czech Republic*, compound interest was rejected on the ground that the 'generous' interest at a rate of 10 per cent would already fully repair the damage incurred by the delay. *CME v Czech Republic*, Final Award on Damages of 14 March 2003, para 643.

would be just and reasonable to award Claimants simple pre-award and post-award interest compounded annually'.[374]

It can be concluded that compound interest is now broadly accepted in international investment practice, though not entirely uniformly. As the applicable rules and legal principles leave a rather larger margin of discretion to tribunals as regards the determination of interest, there will remain some unpredictability in this respect.

2 *Post-award Interest*

Post-award interest is not always distinguished from pre-award interest. In many cases, pre-award interest is simply awarded until the date of payment.[375] However, the function of post-award interest is slightly different and goes beyond the mere compensation for the delay in payment. This is sometimes regarded as a matter of procedural law.[376]

Most importantly, at the date of the award, the dispute about the amount of compensation or damages is settled and there can be no doubt any more about the obligation to the payment. The respondent is in default, if it does not fulfil this obligation. Post-award interest thus serves also as incentive for quick compliance. To this effect it can be higher than pre-award interest and help to combat late payment.[377] It can also have shorter compounding intervals,

374 *Yukos v Russia*, Award of 18 July 2014, para 1689.

375 See, for example, *Técnicas Medioambientales v Mexico*, Award of 29 May 2003, para 197; *Autopista Concesionada de Venezuela v Venezuela*, Award of 23 September 2003, paras 405, 408, 411, and 414; *MTD v Chile*, Award of 25 May 2004, para 250; *S D Myers Inc v Canada*, Second Partial Award of 21 October 2002 (2005) 8 ICSID Reports 124, para 306; *Quasar de Valores v Russia*, Award of 20 July 2012, para 228; *Mobil Cerro Negro v Venezuela*, Award of 9 October 2014, para 404; *Tidewater v Venezuela*, above (n 129) para 217.

376 Also the ILC distinguished it post-award interest from pre-award interest as 'a matter of procedure' and did not deal with it in the context of its Article on State Responsibility. The Commentary in this respect says: 'Article 38 does not deal with post-judgment or moratory interest. It is only concerned with interest that goes to make up the amount that a court or tribunal should award, i.e. compensatory interest. The power of a court or tribunal to award postjudgment interest is a matter of procedure.' See the ILC Commentary, above (n 32) 239.

377 See, for example, the Directive 2011/7/ EU of the European Parliament and of the Council on combating late payment in commercial transactions which sets 'default interest' at a rate which is at least eight percentage points above the reference rate. Article 2(6) of the Directive 2011/7/EU of the European Parliament and of the Council on combating late payment in commercial transactions of 16 February 2011, [2011] OJ L48/ 1.

which has the same effect.[378] In some cases, pre-award interest was awarded as simple interest, but post-award interest should be compounded.[379]

Furthermore, the fulfilment of the payment obligation still lies in the future so that it is not clear how much interest will eventually accrue. While pre-award interest could be calculated as an aggregate amount and be added to the principal (which should be done more often for the benefit of clarity and ease of enforcement),[380] this is not possible with regard to post-award interest.

As regards the *dies a quo* it seems logical that it is the date of the award. However, it is possible that a 'grace period' of several days is free of interest to enable the respondent to arrange the payment, which provides an additional incentive for quick compliance.[381]

In some cases, tribunals decided that they did not have jurisdiction to decide on post-award interest, because they were not explicitly claimed.[382] In order to avoid such a situation, claimants are well-advised to include them in their statement of claim.

XIII Conclusion

The discussion of damages and interest in investment arbitration involves numerous challenges and is likely to remain an interesting topic in the future. Despite considerable progress in the past years with respect to a more general acceptance of the applicable legal principles and economic valuation methods, many details remain subject to debate. As valuation is 'neither the science that some of its proponents make it out to be nor the objective search

378 *Emilio Agustín Maffezini v Spain*, Award of 13 November 2000, paras 96–97; *Metalclad v Mexico*, Award of 30 August 2000, para 131; See also Dolgoff and Duarte-Silva, above, (n 307) 114; Uchkunova and Temnikov, above (n 307) 652, 668.

379 *CMS v Argentina*, Award of 12 May 2005, para 471; *Yukos v Russia*, Award of 18 July 2014, paras 1689–1692.

380 Marboe, *Calculation*, above (n 2) 337–338.

381 See, for example, *Metalclad v Mexico*, Award of 30 August 2000, para 131; *Wena Hotels v Egypt*, Award of 8 December 2000, para 130; *LG&E v Argentina*, Award of 25 July 2007, para 115; *CMS v Argentina*, Award of 12 May 2005, para 471; *Siag v Egypt*, Award of 1 July 2009, para 631(VI)(b); *Rosinvest v Russia*, Award of 22 September 2010, para 43; *Yukos v Russia*, Award of 18 July 2014, para 1691.

382 *Enron v Argentina*, Award of 22 May 2007, para 452; *Sempra v Argentina*, Award of 28 September 2007, para 485.

for true value that idealist would like it to become'[383], there will not be simple solutions suitable for all cases. Tribunals rightfully enjoy discretion in order to apply the relevant principles and methods in each particular case.

However, some consistency and predictability should remain an achievable goal. Some core issues have crystallized in the past years and are becoming accepted more broadly, from the perspective of future claimants or respondents alike. These include the distinction of expropriation from other treaty standards and contractual obligations. While the latter involve remedying wrongful state acts, the former is a distinct feature of state sovereignty. A different standard of compensation is the logical consequence, namely an objective valuation, based on the (fair) market value at the time of the expropriation. In other cases, different valuation approaches are possible and the concrete damage incurred should be the focus in the assessment of quantum. The prevalent aim is to achieve full reparation of the damage incurred. This includes the avoidance of under and over-compensation.

As regards the valuation date, the international law on state responsibility puts restitution as the primary remedy. Some IIAs reverse this priority and set financial compensation first. In any case, the availability of restitution provides an important yardstick for the valuation of damages, including the setting of the valuation date.

The principle of full reparation also includes compensation for non-material damage. The increased acceptance in principle in investor-state arbitration of this item of damages has not yet lead to convincing results in practice. Unlike other international courts and tribunals, investment tribunals put a very high threshold for them. This is particularly disturbing in cases in which the claimant has prevailed on the merits. An option to remedy the wrong incurred would be to award all costs accumulated in years of national and international litigation. This is, however, not yet accepted in practice either.

Full reparation is also the most important rationale for awarding interest. The significant impact the setting of an interest rate has on the amount of money awarded is still not appropriately taken into account in investor-state disputes. Adding a premium of two or four percentage points over LIBOR is a rather widespread practice, but frequently applied without further explanation. The phasing out of LIBOR announced for 2021 will probably be an occasion of reflecting more thoroughly on the choice of the interest rate in international investment arbitration.

---

383 Damodaran, *Investment Valuation* (n 206) 2.

Bibliography

Abdala, Manuel and Spiller, Pablo, 'Chorzów's Standard Rejuvenated: Assessing Damages in Investment Treaty Arbitration', 15 Journal of International Arbitration (2008) 103–120.

Abdala, Manuel, Zadicoff, Pablo López and Spiller, Pablo, 'Invalid Round Trips in Setting Pre-Judgment Interest in International Arbitration', 5 World Arbitration and Mediation Review (2011) 1.

Ahee, Linda, Giacchino, Leonardo and Walck, Rory, 'Historical Analysis of ICSID Concluded Cases' 5 World Arbitration and Mediation Review (2011) 43.

AICPA (ed.), *Statement of Standards on Valuation Services* (American Institute for Certified Public Accountants, New York 2015).

Alexandrov, Stanimir, 'The Present and Future of Moral Damages in Investment Arbitration' in Sabahi, Birch, Laird, and Rivas (eds), *Revolution in the International Rule of Law. Essays in Honour of Don Wallace, Jr* (Juris 2014) 515.

Baginska, Ewa (ed), *Damages for Violations of Human Rights. A Comparative Study of Domestic Legal Systems* (Springer International Publishing 2016).

Beeley, Mark and Walck, Rory, 'Approaches to the Award on Interest by Arbitration Tribunals', 1(1) Journal of Damages in International Arbitration (2014) 51–76.

Beharry, Christina, 'Lawful versus Unlawful Expropriation. Heads I Win, Tails You Lose', 3(1) Journal on Damages in International Arbitration (2016) 57–97.

Binder, Christina 'Necessity Exceptions, the Argentine Crisis and Legitimacy Concerns: or the Benefits of a Public International Law Approach to Investment Arbitration' in Treves and others (eds), *Foreign Investment, International Law and Common Concerns* (Routledge 2014) 71–85.

Birch, Nicholas, 'Curing Uncompensated Expropriation under Chorzów', 3(2) Journal of Damages in International Arbitration (2016) 73–95.

Bjorklund, Andrea, Laird, Ian and Ripinsky, Sergey (eds), *Investment Treaty Law. Current Issues* III (BIICL 2009).

Bollecker-Stern, Brigitte, *Le préjudice dans la théorie de la responsabilité internationale* (Pédone 1973).

Brower, Charles and Brueschke, Juergen, *The Iran–US Claims Tribunal* (Martinus Nijhoff 1999).

Brown, Chester, *Commentaries on Selected Model Investment Treaties* (Oxford University Press 2013).

Bungenberg, Mark, Griebel, Jörn, Hobe, Stephan and Reinisch, August (eds), *International Investment Law. A Handbook* (Beck-Hart-Nomos 2015).

Burgstaller, Markus and Ketcheson, Jonathan, 'Should Expropriation Risk Be Taken Into Account in the Assessment of Damages', 31 ICSID Review-Foreign Investment Law Journal (2016) 193.

Colón, Jeffrey and Knoll, Michael, 'Prejudgment Interest in International Arbitration' (2007) TDM 4(6), www.transnational-dispute-management.com.

Crawford, James, 'Investment Arbitration and the ILC Articles on State Responsibility', 25 ICSID Review-Foreign Investment Law Journal (2010) 127.

Crawford, James, *Brownlie's Principles of International Law* (Oxford University Press 2012).

Crawford, James, Pellet, Allain and Olleson, Simon (eds), *The Law of International Responsibility* (Oxford University Press 2009).

Damodaran, Aswath, *Investment Valuation: Tools and Techniques for Determining the Value of Any Asset* (3rd edn, Wiley 2012).

Dolgoff, Aaron and Duarte-Silva, Tiago, 'Prejudgment Interest: An Economic Review of Alternative Approaches', 33 Journal of International Arbitration (2016) 99–114.

Dolzer, Rudolf and Schreuer, Christoph, *Principles of International Investment Law* (2nd edn, Oxford University Press 2012).

Dolzer, Rudolf 'Indirect Expropriations: New Developments?', 11 *NYU Environmental Law Journal* (2002–2003) 64–93.

Dorobantu, Florin, Dupont, Natasha and Maniatis, Alexis, 'Country Risk and Damages in Investment Arbitration', 31 ICSID Review-Foreign Investment Law Journal (2016) 219–231.

Douglas, Zachary, 'Other Specific Regimes of Responsibility: Investment Treaty Arbitration and ICSID' in Crawford, Pellet and Olleson (eds), *The Law of International Responsibility* (Oxford University Press 2009) 815.

Douglas, Zachary, Pauwelyn, Joost and Viñuales, Jorge (eds), *International Investment Law. Bringing Theory Into Practice* (Oxford University Press 2014).

Dumberry, Patrick, 'Compensation for Moral Damages in Investor-State Arbitration Disputes', 27 Journal of International Arbitration (2010) 247.

Dumberry, Patrick, 'Moral Damages' in Bungenberg, Griebel, Hobe and Reinisch (eds), *International Investment Law. A Handbook* (Beck-Hart-Nomos 2015) 1130.

Fishman, Jay, Pratt, Shannon and Morrison, William, *Standards of Value* (2nd edn, Wiley 2013).

Fraser, Alexander and Aaron, Sheryl, 'End of LIBOR in UK: Impact on Loan Documents and Swaps', The National Law Review of 8 August 2017, see https://www.natlawreview.com/article/end-libor-uk-impact-loan-documents-and-swaps.

Gazzini, Tarcisio and de Brabandere, Eric (eds), *International Investment Law: The Sources of Rights and Obligations* (Martinus Nijhoff 2012).

Gazzini, Tarcisio, 'Bilateral Investment Treaties', in Gazzini and de Brabandere (eds), *International Investment Law: The Sources of Rights and Obligations* (Martinus Nijhoff 2012) 99.

Giacchino, Leonardo and Sturma, Pavel, 'Trends in Awards from Concluded ICSID Cases', 4(2) Journal on Damages in International Arbitration (2017) 51.

Goodman, Ronald and Parkhomenko, Yuri, 'Does the *Chorzów Factory* Standard Apply in Investment Arbitration? A Contextual Reappraisal' 32 ICSID Review-Foreign Investment Law Journal (2017) 304–325.

Gotanda, John and Walck, Rory, 'Editors' Note' 1 Journal of Damages in International Arbitration (2014) v.

Gotanda, John, 'A Study of Interest' Villanova University School of Law/Public Law and Legal Theory Working Paper No. 2007–10 (August 2007).

Gotanda, John, 'Awarding Interest in International Arbitration', 90 AJIL (1996) 40.

Gotanda, John, 'Compound Interest in International Disputes' Oxford University Comparative Law Forum (2004) 2.

Gotanda, John, 'Interest' in Bungenberg and others (eds), *International Investment Law. A Handbook* (Beck-Hart-Nomos 2015) 1142–1153.

Gotanda, John, 'Recovering Lost Profits in International Disputes' 36 Georgetown Journal of International Law (2004) 61.

Gotanda, John, *Supplemental Damages in Private International Law* (Kluwer Law International 1997).

Herdegen, Matthias, *Principles of International Economic Law* (Oxford University Press 2013).

ICCA-ASIL Task Force on Damages, available at http://www.arbitration-icca.org/projects/ICCA-ASIL-Task-Force-on-Damages.html (20 August 2017).

International Law Commission, Draft Articles on Responsibility of States for Internationally Wrongful Acts, with commentaries, *Yearbook of the International Law Commission*, vol. II, Part Two (2001).

IVSC, *International Valuation Standards 2013* (International Valuation Standards Council 2013).

Jagusch, Stephen and Sebastian, Thomas, 'Moral Damages in Investment Arbitration: Punitive Damages in Contemporary Clothing', 29 Journal of International Arbitration (2012) 45.

Kantor, Mark, 'The Limitations of Arbitration' 1(2) TDM (2004) www.transnational-dispute-management.com.

Kantor, Mark, 'Fifty billion Dollars. The Yukos Damages Awards', 2(1) Journal on Damages in International Arbitration (2015) 91–149.

Kantor, Mark, *Valuation for Arbitration* (Alphen aan den Rijn: Kluwer Law International, 2008).

Khachvani, David, 'Compensation for Unlawful Expropriation: Targeting the Illegality' 32 ICSID Review-Foreign Investment Law Journal (2017) 385.

Koller, Tim, Goedhart, Mark and Wessels, David, *Valuation: Measuring and Managing the Value of Companies* (6th edn, Wiley & Sons 2015).

Kriebaum, Ursula, 'Expropriation', in Bungenberg, Griebel, Hobe and Reinisch, *International Investment Law. A Handbook* (Beck-Hart-Nomos 2015) 959.

Lauterpacht, Elihu and Nevill, Penelope, 'Interest' in Crawford, Pellet, and Olleson (eds), *The Law of International Responsibility* (Oxford University Press, 2010) 613–622.

Lavaud, Floriane and Costa, Guilherme Recenta, 'Valuation Date in Investment Arbitration: A Fundamental Examination of Chorzów's Principles, 3(2) Journal of Damages in International Arbitration (2016) 33–72.

Leal-Arcas, Rafael, *International Trade and Investment Law. Multilateral, Regional and Bilateral Governance* (Edward Elgar 2010) 187–190.

Mann, F A, 'Compound Interest as an Item of Damages in International Law' UC Davis Law Review (1988) 540.

Marboe, Irmgard, 'State Responsibility and Comparative State Liability for Administrative and Legislative Harm to Economic Interests', in Schill (ed), *International Investment Law and Comparative Public Law* (Oxford University Press 2010) 377.

Marboe, Irmgard, *Calculation of Compensation and Damages in Investment Arbitration* (2nd edn, Oxford University Press 2017).

Marboe, Irmgard, Compensation and Damages in International Law. The Limits of "Fair Market Value", 7 Journal of World Investment and Trade (2006) 723–760.

Miles, Craig and Weiss, David, 'Overview of Principles Reducing Damages' in Trenor (ed), *Guide to Damages* (GAR Publications 2017) 78.

Mommsen, Friedrich, *Lehre von dem Interesse* (Schetschke und Sohn 1855).

Montt, Santiago, *State Liability in Investment Treaty Arbitration. Global Constitutional and Administrative Law in the BIT Generation* (Hart 2009).

Muchlinsky, Peter, Ortino, Federico and Schreuer, Christoph (eds), *The Oxford Handbook of International Investment Law* (Oxford University Press 2008).

Norton, Patrick 'A Law of the Future or a Law of the Past? Modern Tribunals and the International Law of Expropriation', 85 AJIL (1991) 474, 479.

Paparinskis, Martins, 'Investment Treaty Arbitration and the (New) Law of State Responsibility', 24 EJIL (2013) 617.

Paulsson, Jan, 'The Expectation Model' in Derains and Kreindler (eds), *Evaluation of Damages in International Arbitration* (International Chamber of Commerce 2006) 57.

Pratt, Shannon and Niculita, Alina, *The Lawyer's Business Valuation Handbook* (2nd edn, ABA).

Pratt, Shannon and Niculita, Alina, *Valuing a Business. The Analysis and Appraisal of Closely Held Companies* (5th edn, McGraw-Hill 2008).

PricewaterhouseCoopers, 2015, 'International Arbitration Damages Research—Closing the Gap between Claimants and Respondents', available at http://www.pwc.co.uk/services/forensic-services/disputes/2015-internationalarbitration-damages-research-closingthe-gap-between-claimants-and-respondents.html; reprinted in 3(1) Journal of Damages in International Arbitration (2016) 99.

Puig, Sergio, 'No Right Without a Remedy: Foundations of Investor-State Arbitration', in Douglas, Pauwelyn, and Viñuales (eds), *International Investment Law. Bringing Theory Into Practice* (Oxford University Press 2014) 235.

Quick, Reinhard, 'Why TTIP Should Have an Investment Chapter Including ISDS', 49 Journal of World Trade (2015) 199–209.

Ratner, Steven, 'Compensation for Expropriations in a World of Investment Treaties: Beyond the Lawful/Unlawful Distinction' 111 AJIL (2017) 7–56.

Reinisch, August (ed), *Standards of Investment Protection* (Oxford University Press 2008).

Reinisch, August, 'Austria', in Brown, *Commentaries on Selected Model Investment Treaties* (Oxford University Press 2013) 15.

Reinisch, August, 'Expropriation' in Muchlinski, Ortino and Schreuer (eds), *The Oxford Handbook of International Investment Law* (Oxford University Press 2008) 407.

Reinisch, August, 'Legality of Expropriations' in Reinisch (ed) *Standards of Investment Protection* (Oxford University Press 2008) 171.

Reinisch, August, 'Necessity in Investment Arbitration' 41 Netherlands Yearbook of International Law (2010), 137–158.

Ribeiro, Clarisse (ed), *Investment Arbitration and the Energy Charter Treaty* (JurisNet LLC 2006).

Ripinsky, Sergey and Williams, Kevin, *Damages in International Investment Law* (British Institute of International and Comparative Law 2008).

Sabahi, Borzu and Duggal, Kabir, 'Occidental Petroleum v Ecuador (2012). Observations on Proportionality, Assessment of Damages and Contributory Fault' 28 ICSID Review-Foreign Investment Law Journal (2013) 279.

Sabahi, Borzu, Birch, Nicholas, Laird, Ian and Rivas, José Antonio (eds), *Revolution in the International Rule of Law. Essays in Honour of Don Wallace, Jr* (Juris 2014) 515.

Sabahi, Borzu, *Compensation and Restitution in Investor-State Arbitration. Principles and Practice* (Oxford University Press 2011).

Sabahi, Borzu, Duggal, Kabir and Birch, Nicholas, 'Limits on Compensation for Internationally Wrongful Acts' in Bungenberg, Griebel, Hobe, and Reinisch (eds), *International Investment Law. A Handbook* (Beck-Hart-Nomos 2015) 1115.

Salacuse, Jeswald, *The Three Laws of International Investment* (Oxford University Press 2013) 355.

Schill, Stephan (ed), *International Investment Law and Comparative Public Law* (Oxford University Press 2010).

Schill, Stephan, *The Multilateralization of International Investment Law* (Cambridge University Press 2009).

Schreuer, Christoph and others, *The ICSID Convention: A Commentary*, (2nd edn, Cambridge University Press 2009).

Schreuer, Christoph, 'Alternative Remedies in Investment Arbitration', 3(1) Journal of Damages in International Arbitration (2016) 1.

Schwarzenberger, Georg, *International Law as Applied by International Tribunals* (Stevens and Sons 1957).

Sénéchal, Thierry and Gotanda, John, 'Interest as Damages', 47 Columbia Journal of Transnational Law (2009) 491.

Sénéchal, Thierry, 'Time Value of Money: A Case Study' 4(6) TDM (2007), www.transnational-dispute-management.com.

Shaw, Malcolm, *International Law* (8th edn, Cambridge University Press 2017).

Shelton, Dinah, *Remedies in International Human Rights Law* (2nd edn, Oxford University Press 2005).

Sheppard, Audrey, 'The Distinction between Lawful and Unlawful Expropriation', in Ribeiro (ed), *Investment Arbitration and the Energy Charter Treaty* (JurisNet LLC 2006) 169.

Smith, Mick and Vikis, Romans, 'Whose Money is it and Should it Matter? An Essay on the Cost of Capital in International Arbitration', 10(4) TDM (2013).

Sorenson, Max (ed), *Manual of Public International Law* (Macmillan 1968).

Sornarajah, Muthucumaraswamy, *The International Law of Foreign Investment*, (3rd edn, Cambridge University Press 2010).

Spielermann, Ole, 'Applicable Law', in Muchlinsky, Ortino, Schreuer (eds), *The Oxford Handbook of International Investment Law* (Oxford University Press 2008) 89.

Taniguchi, Yasuhei, 'The Obligation to Mitigate Damages' in Derains and Kreindler (eds), *Evaluation of Damages in International Arbitration* (International Chamber of Commerce 2006) 79.

Titi, Catherine, 'The European Union's Proposal for an International Investment Court: Significance, Innovations and Challenges Ahead', TDM 1 (2017) www.transnational-dispute-management.com.

Trenor, John A., (ed), *The Guide to Damages in International Arbitration* (Global Arbitration Review 2016).

Treves, Tullio and others (eds), *Foreign Investment, International Law and Common Concerns* (Routledge 2014).

Uchkunova, Inna and Temnikov, Oleg, 'A Procrustean Bed: Pre- and Post-Award Interest in ICSID Arbitration' 29 ICSID Review-Foreign Investment Law Journal (2014) 648–668.

UNCTAD, *World Investment Report 2015. Reforming International Investment Governance* (United Nations 2015) 116.

v Harten, Gus and Loughlin, Martin, 'Investment Treaty Arbitration as a Species of Global Administrative Law', 17 EJIL (2006) 121.

Vandevelde, Kenneth, *Bilateral Investment Treaties. History, Politics, and Interpretation* (Oxford University Press 2010).

Waelde, Thomas and Sabahi, Borzu, 'Compensation, Damages, and Valuation' in Muchlinski and others (eds), *The Oxford Handbook of International Investment Law* (Oxford University Press 2008) 1049.

Whiteman, Majorie, *Damages in International Law, vol. III* (Government Printing Office, Washington 1943).

Whiteman, Majorie, *Digest of International Law, vol. III* (Government Printing Office, Washington 1967).

Wittich, Stephan, 'Non-Material Damage and Monetary Reparation in International Law' 15 Finish Yearbook of International Law (2004) 329.

Wittich, Stephan, 'Punitive Damages', in Crawford, Pellet, and Olleson (eds), *The Law of International Responsibility* (Oxford University Press 2010) 667.

World Bank, 'Legal Framework for the Treatment of Foreign Investment' (1992) 31 ILM 1363.

World Bank, *Legal Framework for the Treatment of Foreign Investment, Vol. 2, Report to the Development Committee and Guidelines on the Treatment of Foreign Direct Investment* (World Bank Group, Washington 1992).

Wöss, Herfried, San Román Rivera, Adriana, Spiller, Pablo, and Dellepiane, Santiago, *Damages in International Arbitration Under Complex Long-Term Contracts* (Oxford University Press 2014).

www.ingramcontent.com/pod-product-compliance
Lightning Source LLC
Chambersburg PA
CBHW031331230926
51848CB00001B/191
* 9 7 8 9 0 0 4 3 6 6 8 5 5 *